D1260251

THE DOUBLE LIFE
OF
J. M. W. TURNER

TURNER AT 27

SELF-PORTRAIT

(*National Gallery*)

The
DOUBLE LIFE
of
J. M. W. TURNER

By
KENELM FOSS

"O world invisible, we view thee,
O world intangible, we touch thee,
O world unknowable, we know thee,
Inapprehensible, we clutch thee!"

FRANCIS THOMPSON

London
MARTIN SECKER
Publisher to The Richards Press
8 Charles Street
St. James's Square
1938

LONDON: THE RICHARDS PRESS LTD.

FOREWORD

THE standard biographies of this outstanding genius were written in Victorian times, and are Victorian in manner and nauseatingly so in moral inference. While grudgingly admitting that Turner was the greatest landscape-seascape painter of all time, they suggest that it happened in spite of the fact that he was mean, unsociable, unwashed, intemperate, and the father of at least five illegitimate children. It would seem to the present writer more logical to say that a man was an artist of inspired vision in spite of the fact that he was a much-respected suburban ratepayer, a popular member of the Borough Council, a staunch chapel-goer, teetotaller, and non-smoker, who never missed the 8.5 to the city each morning.

They likewise deplore the fact that this immortal was no gentleman.

My book is not about a gentleman, but about a man; and about a man so single-minded that he devoted the whole of his life to one unselfish purpose. By denying himself all his days he left behind him a fortune of £140,000 (equalling half a million of money to-day) obtained not through investment, but by the labour of his hands, to assist brother-artists less fortunately placed than himself. That is an achievement no one else can claim; any more than they can bequeath freely to posterity, as he did, imperishable work of unimaginable beauty.

Hampstead, 1938.   K. F.

v

CONTENTS

LIST OF ILLUSTRATIONS

THE DOUBLE LIFE
OF J. M. W. TURNER

CHAPTER I

1770–85

THE streets of London in the early 1770's were doubtless paved with gold to much the same extent as
nowadays, but the scarcity of scavengers and chimney-
sweeps then, as well as the volume of foot- and horse-
traffic, gave them an additional crust of mud and
grime. The bearers of sedan-chairs, the watchmen
and hackney-coachmen, jostled each other for the
most part in streets wheel-rutted like a farm-track,
with overflowing gutters thick in refuse. Just such a
throughfare was Maiden, or Midden, Lane, a narrow
causeway running parallel with the Strand from
Covent Garden to 'the full tide of existence' at Charing
Cross. It was to this unpromising jumping-off ground
that, round about 1770, when Captain Cook was
discovering New South Wales, one William Turner,
a barber and peruke-maker by trade, came from
South Molton, Devonshire, to make his fortune.

  The spot was a good one as regards theatrical
connection, being then, as now, in close proximity to
a number of play-houses, and about midway between

two of the most fashionable, the Haymarket and
Drury Lane. Apart from the stage, however, wigs
were at that period almost universally worn, those of
the 'cascade' variety costing as much as fifty guineas
each. A man of any quality would own three—one
for day use, and the other two, elaborately powdered,
for, respectively, evenings, and Sundays, hey-days and
holidays. Boswell, writing busily just then, tells us
that even someone so careless of appearances as Dr.
Johnson kept customarily two wigs, a 'curt Busby'
for everyday wear—mutilated, we are told, 'by reading
a-bed, as was his constant custom', so that 'the
foretops of all his wigs were burned by the candle
down to the very network'—and a better one, in the
custody of Mrs. Thrale's butler at Streatham, into
which the Doctor on his frequent visits was assisted
as soon as the dinner-bell rang.

William Turner, sitting dressing a peruke in his
unpretentious shop-door at No. 26 Maiden Lane, must
often have seen the great lexicographer pass in his
worsted stockings and brown surtout on his way from
his lodgings in Bolt Court to the Literary Club held at
Old Slaughter's Coffee-House, in St. Martin's Lane.
The *Talkers'* Club, the gossips of that period called
it, seeing that its principal members were the silvery-
tongued Edmund Burke and his brother-politician,
the persuasive, reckless Charles James Fox; foppish
Topham Beauclerk (who nevertheless 'stank', according to Horace Walpole); sawny, snobbish Sir Joshua
Reynolds, with his high white wig, silver buckles, red

12

scarred face, gold snuff-box and ear-trumpet; Oliver Goldsmith, 'who wrote like an angel and talked like Poor Poll', either down-at-heel or in gaudy finery, according to the state of his finances; and the chirruping Scotch sparrow Boswell, waiting upon the lightest word of the pompous, gouty, rough, irascible, sixty-one-year-old Dr. Johnson, and his 'bow-wow way', queer rolling gait, and faithful negro servant ever in attendance.

Though the gay-striped barber's pole and bulging shop-window of the elder Turner's saloon faced Maiden Lane, as did the ramshackle, mean rooms above, the actual entrance was in Hand Court. The premises were demolished in 1821, but Ruskin describes how a customer had to leave the Lane through a narrow archway with an iron gate, and enter the shop by way of a coffin-lid door on the left-hand side of the dark court. The show-case facing the street must have displayed primitive barber's dummies sporting bob and cauliflower wigs, more or less in the fashion of theatrical costumiers of to-day. But there the resemblance to modern times ceased, for contemporary writers, describing coiffeur-shops 'on Change', mention 'braiding pins fourteen inches long, powder bags, crisping-irons, leather rolls for forming curls, and spiral machines for frizzing the hair'—the latter an unpatented fore-runner, obviously, of the paraphernalia needed for producing a 'permanent' wave in 1938.

Barber Turner, as all accounts agree, was a cheery little fellow, talkative ('the badge of all his tribe') in a nasal voice, with pronounced Devonshire twang. Stumpy and muscular, fresh complexioned, with beady, bright-blue eyes in a smallish head, he had the parrot-nose and projecting chin of Mr. Punch, features causing the epithet 'Jewish' to be as frequently applied to him as to his celebrated son, who inherited his physical characteristics. But I can find evidence of Hebraic strain neither in the barber father nor in the woman he was to marry shortly after reaching London.

The inference may have arisen through the combination of the family's undeniably beaky nasal organ, and their equally indubitable tendency to be rather more than near in money-matters. But of that more anon. Turner senior was a thrifty, conscientious, hard-working 'character', and certainly had the gift of pleasing his customers, many of whom—distinguished men among them—are known to have treated him more as a friend than a tradesman. Not only was Maiden Lane frequented by celebrated theatrical managers like the elderly, diminutive, cheese-paring David Garrick, and the quick-witted, slanderous, one-legged Samuel Foote, 'ever tee-hee-ing', but famous authors also, like handsome, devil-may-care Irish Sheridan, *bon vivant* and Corinthian, or "Decline and Fall" Edward Gibbon, with his huge belly, tiny feet, and reedy, high pitched, old maid's voice. For the locality, though a backwater, was one in the centre of culture. Milton's secretary, Andrew Marvell, known as 'the incorruptible patriot', had lived there:

14

for two years the fretful Voltaire had lodged at 'The White Perruke', and, in the 1770's, with which we are concerned, 'an artist-colony met, where the cider cellar formerly stood', the great Sir Joshua's studio was hard by, in Leicester Fields: Gainsborough was in Pall Mall, where he painted his Duchesses of Devonshire, and the Royal Academy headquarters were at Somerset House.

It was an age rich in genius, if troublous politically, that reign of George III—'Farmer George', as his affectionate subjects loved to call him. For popular he undoubtedly was, through all the loss of the American Colonies and the war with France, right up to the time of his becoming palpably demented. Until then, the vast bulk of his faithful subjects did not give a fig for his broken English, or laugh at him either for having fifteen children, or for spending his evenings at home, over the backgammon board, sipping lemonade. They positively admired his domestic traits, so vindictively lampooned by Gillray, such as toasting his own muffins, frying sprats, and stopping while hunting to ask the old countrywoman how the apple got into the dumpling.

It was a London of contrasts, where the bucks were gamesters, losing £70,000 in a night at Almack's in dicing or at faro, over a hogshead of claret, or inspired by bowls of 'the liquor called Bishop': while not far away there still existed ducking-stools for scolds, pillories where unpopular malefactors were oft-times stoned to death by the mob, and convict-hulks upon the Thames. Though the theft of more than a shillingsworth was punishable by death, though women were still being publicly burned at Tyburn, the lucrative trade of smuggling was winked at, and negro slaves were openly sold for shipment to Sierra Leone under conditions of unspeakable brutality and degradation. The heads of malefactors stood exposed on Temple Bar, warning all wandering marauders from there to Fleet Ditch that there were trained-bands with swords and muskets for the suppression of crime. Whether he journeyed a-horseback to Twickenham or by post-chaise to Brighthelmstone, a traveller must be armed against highwaymen, one of whose happy hunting-grounds was Streatham Common.

The press-gang found the Navy its men; coals were 7*d*. per cwt.; and the novel doctrines of Methodism were first being spread by the unhappily-married brothers Wesley. In the House of Commons, under the leadership of Lord North, Members were accustomed to crack nuts, eat oranges, lie upon the benches, retire into the galleries for a doze, and weep copiously and in unison at any moving flight of oratory. One took a ferry at Temple Stairs to cross to Blackfriars; and charges were reckoned in multiples or fractions of the guinea—dancing lessons being quoted in the Public Prints at 5*s*. 3*d*. per half-hour session. A shilling then equalled 3*s*. 6*d*. to-day.

Elegant ladies in sacques and ruffles, hoops and patches, (who '*even* put on rouge' on occasion, as

Fanny Burney, a contemporary, quaintly observes) would sit at the distaff, the tambour-frame, or the spinet, and take a dish of tea or chocolate, seated on petit-point, beneath crystal chandeliers. And you may be sure that amidst the stately periods of their decorous conversation would occur such phrases as 'monstrous', 'vastly' and 'prodigious'. The sleeping-apartments (referred to even more rarely than 'breeches', 'unmentionables', and 'small-clothes') were invariably bed-chambers, up two or more pairs of stairs. In sickness, an apothecary was called in, who, during convalescence, might recommend Florence wine, nonpareils, or sweetmeats.

In the busy streets, crowded with horsemen, loaded porters, Bow Street runners, vendors of lavender and spruce, town-criers, and noblemen's phaetons embla-zoned with coats of arms, the tailors sat cross-legged in their windows, the bookshops lacked glass fronts so that customers could browse undisturbed; while in the coffee-shops a goodman might peruse his Morning Chronicle or Post and take a pinch of rappee in peace. The pewterer plied his trade next the tallow-chandler or the pickle shop; the bed-rooms of the coaching-inns were reached by outside galleries; and a glance within the Mitre Tavern, or almost any ale-house, showed the turnspit, perchance somewhat in liquor, preparing the house's One-Shilling Ordinary, con-sisting of some such trifle as—Broth, Boiled Leg of Mutton and Spinach, a Sweetmeat or Veal Pie, and Pudding. And for evening entertainment there was

B

17

the Pantheon; that 'splendid place of public amusement', Ranelagh, with its raree-shows; or Torrè's
Fireworks in the Marylebone Gardens; the annual
Gooseberry Fair in Tottenham Court Road, and the
perennial "Beggar's Opera".

The heavy-pillared portico of St. Paul's Church,
Covent Garden (then recently immortalised by
Hogarth: and providing Bernard Shaw, nearly a
century and a half later, with a setting for the first
act of his "Pygmalion") stood facing the Vegetable
Market, just as it does now. The Parish Register for
1773 has an entry that on August 29th William
Turner, Bachelor, married Mary Ann Mallad (or
Mallord?), Spinster, of Islington.

The fact that the lady boasted, literally boasted,
relationship with the Marshall family of Shelford
Manor, Nottingham, has led some writers to give her
maiden name as Marshall, but the fact that the
unusual Mallord in Joseph Mallord William Turner's
name came from his mother is as patent as that the
lady, however aristocratically connected, was employed
as a housekeeper immediately prior to her marriage
with the barber. Her sister, however, as she was
wont to point out, had married the Rev. Mr. Harpur,
Curate of Islington.

The home that the barber took her to in Maiden
Lane was noisy, small, and dingy, the rooms poky
and low-ceilinged, dark, and reached by stairs that
were steep and winding. Indeed, it would seem that
the couple's principal—and subsequently their only—

living-room was the basement-kitchen. Cellar-kitchen, say most accounts, but we learn that it at least was lighted by a window raised partially above pavement-level, and not solely through an area-grating. Nevertheless, it was all doubtless unduly trying to the ex-housekeeper descendant of the Shelford Marshalls, and may conceivably have contributed to her outstanding characteristic then and subsequently—the possession of an ungovernable temper, which was to lead her hard-working husband such a sorry dance that it needed all his obstinate good humour to withstand it.

She was a little woman, somewhat masculine in aspect, and always holding herself forbiddingly erect. Her famous son made a youthful portrait of her, wearing a cap with large flappers over her elaborately frizzed hair, the lower lip projecting, the eyes pale blue, the nose beaky as her husband's. To the barber's Punch she must have been a fitting Judy, in appearance at least. But contrasting with his provincial solid sense, there were in her the seeds of insanity, of which her shrewish ragings were the first indication—ending in complete dementia and her death in Bethlehem (alias Bedlam) Hospital. But this, like every other real-life tragedy, was not immediate and dramatic, but unendurably long-drawn-out, with removals to and from her home in hope renewed and lost again, until the unhappy ending.

It seems a fitting moment, however, to reflect that her famous son's undeniable eccentricity of character, and possibly in part his genius, may have sprung from the mental instability of his mother. We have no proof that he bore anything but affection for her, and plenty of evidence that, with the sensibility of an artist, he resented any reference to her, both in boyhood and in later life, and brusquely silenced queries regarding her. From her, as well as from his father, he derived his short stature, and not improbably his stinginess as well.

But our hero is not yet born, though the stage is all set for his appearance.

In 1773, the year of the Boston Tea Party which led to the American Revolution, "She Stoops to Conquer" saw the light at Covent Garden under Colman, with Garrick supervising the rehearsals. In the following year its author, Goldsmith, died; Clive of India committed suicide; and Lord Chesterfield's Letters to his Son were published by the son's widow. And in 1775 Sheridan's "Rivals" had its original production; Mrs. Siddons, as Portia, first appeared at Drury Lane; Paul Revere made history with his ride; and on April 23rd (Shakespeare's birthday and St. George's Day) the Maiden Lane barber's wife bore a son, who on May 14th was, at St. Paul's, Covent Garden, baptised Joseph Mallord William Turner, the Joseph being after his mother's eldest brother.

The various accounts of Barber Turner all agree to brand him suspicious and inordinately mean. He is alleged to have run out into the Lane after a customer who had unwittingly not been charged an extra halfpenny for soap; and it is true that when his son in later life was twitted with his own close-fistedness, he sardonically replied: "Well? What can you expect? The only thing Dad ever praised me for was for having saved a halfpenny."

Some scribes also claim that the elder Turner was plumb-ignorant, but on the other hand we learn that it was he who taught the artist to read if not to write. It also seems improbable that anyone who, like the barber, was chiefly notable for his loquacity, and for the quickness of his speech, should be lacking either in ideas or general knowledge of a topical kind.

His one quite indisputable good quality was his abiding affection for his only son, and there is plenty to show that it started with the infant's earliest years. In those days hairdressers 'waited upon gentlemen at their residences' of a morning, to shave them and so forth—visits which Father William continued to pay to certain favoured customers long after his retirement. One can visualise the sprightly little barber arriving with his bag of tongs and scissors, powder, puffs, Macassar oil, and razors, and donning his professional striped jacket. One can see the yawning patron, rendered helpless by the sheet wrapped round him, submitting perforce to the operator's professional small-talk, now newly interspersed, in 1776–7–8, by irrelevant anecdotes regarding his exceptional child.

Chitter-chatter respecting the American Declaration of Independence, for instance, or the success of Mr.

Sheridan's masterly new comedy "The School for Scandal", would be broken off by a chuckled anecdote as to the infant Billy's attraction towards the shaving-brushes—he was evidently cut out to be a barber. Or interest in the Cock Lane Ghost, the death of Chatham, or the anonymous author of the just-published "Evelina", would fade in proud recountal of young Billy's latest feat . . . how he had tried to draw with his finger in spilt milk upon the tea-tray . . . he was surely meant to be an artist, not a barber; or as to what a wonderful 'ead of 'air 'e 'ad.

Other anecdotes relate how Davy Garrick, soon to die, amused the child by posing in the Maiden Lane shop-window as a barber's dummy, a simple feat to one who could 'act a gridiron' if he felt disposed. And as to how it was a traveller in cosmetics who gave the perruquier's son his first lesson in colour, by placing a blob of carmine on a wig-block and gradually working it with the thumb outwards till the tint intermingled with that of the wooden surface.

The first known drawing of the embryonic artist was in 1780, when he was only five. Close by the barber's there was, in Southampton Street, Covent Garden, a prosperous jeweller's kept by a Mr. Tomkison, whom Old Turner used to attend professionally at the shopkeeper's private house in Carburton Street. One day he took the child along with him, and while the father, prattling as ever, curled and crimped the client's hair, young Turner, pardonably agape at the bourgeois magnificence compared

22

with Maiden Lane, tiptoed about, filling his eyes and memory. A silver salver took his fancy (or according to another version, a set of castors), engraved with an heraldic lion rampant in a coat of arms. All next day the queer child was closeted in his attic-bedroom, producing at the end of it an undeniable heraldic lion, duly rampant. He soon, also, commenced to copy engravings, for in Mr. Crooke's copy of Pennant's "London" in the British Museum there is an Interior of Westminster Abbey from the pencil of the precocious boy. The father's pride and pleasure therein is not merely legend, for the son of Stothard, the contemporary artist, has recorded it as a fact that Turner *père* delightedly exhibited the drawing to his customer, the elder Stothard, with the triumphant comment, "My son, too, is going to be a painter!"

Thomas Stothard, incidentally, was the illustrator of Ossian, the true authorship of which was then much agitating Johnson, and indeed the whole literary clique. Residing in Henrietta Street, close by the barber's, Stothard was a circumspect shy creature, unlike the generality of artists of that period. He collected butterflies in order to glean new colour-schemes from their wings; and as a half-starved youth had been taught dancing by the father of Grimaldi, the clown. The young Turner's admiration for the diffident illustrator continued for years, and he was still wont to say "I wish I could paint like Stothard" long after he had outclassed him.

This was the year of Rodney's trouncing of the

Spanish fleet at Cape St. Vincent, a news-scoop, doubtless, for the newly-issued Morning Herald, which presumably did not give equal prominence to the seduction and speedy, unrecompensed desertion of the exquisite Perdita Robinson by George, Prince of Wales, then a promising libertine of eighteen summers. In this year also took place the Lord George Gordon 'No Popery' Riots (afterwards figuring in Dickens' "Barnaby Rudge") wherein, in Dr. Johnson's words, 'the Protestants set fire to the Fleet and to the King's Bench, and I know not how many other places . . . broke open the Marshalsea, the Wood-street Compter, and Clerkenwell Bridewell, and released all the prisoners . . . and, marching to Westminster, insulted the lords and commons, who all bore it with great tameness'. Lord George, incidentally, was acquitted when brought to trial, though many of his followers were executed. He died in Newgate, however, later, after having quaintly become a Jew.

Of Turner at six or seven years old we learn something from an equestrian portrait still extant, which depicts him as a cheerful, even passably handsome, child with chestnut hair, clothed in green with a leather belt, and mounted on a pony. The pony suggests that the otherwise parsimonious barber was already indulgent towards his son. Certain it is that during the next year or two the question of the boy's education had begun to concern him. There were Free Schools then as now, but the idea of that being good enough for the painter-to-be seems not to have

occurred to the devoted parent, who was wont subsequently to plume himself not a little on the good
'eddycation' he had given to his Billy.

Since the boy was delicate, or to doting eyes seemed
delicate, a healthier locality than Central London
must be found, and Brentford was the place selected.
Should that spot not commend itself to the reader as
conspicuously salubrious, he must recollect that it was
then a sylvan riverside retreat, as pastoral as the
adjoining Kew, which had been chosen by domesticated George III as an idyllic country hermitage.
It was, moreover, adjacent to historic Hampton
Court, and the chestnut avenues of Bushy Park;
closer still to Twickenham, where the painter was
later to rusticate, possibly led there by pleasant
memories of childhood.

His fellow-pupils at John White's 'Academy',
opposite the Three Pigeons Tavern at New Brentford
Butts, consisted of ten girls and fifty boys. All were
day-boarders, so young Turner lodged with a maternal
uncle named Marshall, who, for one connected even
remotely with the Shelford Manor Marshalls of
Nottingham, followed the mortifyingly plebeian calling
of a butcher. Former schoolfellows of Turner's used
to relate, after he found fame, that he was wont to
chalk up recognisable cocks and hens upon the play-
ground wall; and how he was for ever 'idling', and
spending class-time sketching surreptitiously whatever
birds and trees and flowers he could see from the
schoolroom window. There were, it appears, always

25

other boys ready to do his lessons for him in exchange for these immature drawings. He did not stay at Brentford long, and his art-impelled neglect of 'book-learning' there and elsewhere accounts for the fact that he never in later life was able properly to write or even to speak his native tongue. Mere illegibility was common (witness his contemporary, Beethoven), but Turner remained sheerly illiterate.

Compensatorily, it was at Brentford, that his first essays in water-colour were made. There is a charming reminiscence of this period, from a schoolgirl contemporary who continued to know him all through his long life, of how as a boy he would scramble up a tree to get a better view, relying on her to hand him any additional material he needed. His earliest extant drawing, a view of Margate Church (for the rampant lion had opened its heraldic wings and vanished), was done at Brentford, and must, one feels, have been a copy, for he is not known to have visited Margate till later. But concrete progress in his career was made during his few months' stay at White's Academy, for one John Lees, a foreman at the Brentford Distillery, hearing of the youth's talent, gave him the tinting, at 4d. a plate, of 140 engravings from Boswell's "Antiquities of England and Wales." The enterprising Lees without question 'builded better than he knew', but the commission had put ideas into the industrious young artist's head. Profiting by his temporary possession of the engravings, he made coloured copies of sundry of them for sale elsewhere.

Shortly afterwards, declared an irremediable dunce by his schoolmaster, he was summoned back to Maiden Lane, and put to earn his bread and salt as lather-boy, sweeping out the shop, running for hot water, etc. etc. But his father, business-like in other ways as well, saw commercial possibilities in the Brentford drawings, and with pride exhibited them—"My son's, sir, at three shillings"—to artist-customers, more than one of whom, approving, declared roundly that he should have the boy properly trained. But artists are not purchasers; and the barber pinned up the juvenile masterpieces outside the entrance-door of his hairdressing-saloon, marking them for what he reckoned they would fetch, the prices asked ranging from one to three shillings apiece. The move was a practical one, being a primitive form of publicity, and was to prove an important step on the ladder of his son's eventual fame.

While the above was happening, Dr. Johnson died; the first mail-coach travelled from London to Bristol and the first balloon ascent was made by Lunardi; the last execution took place at Tyburn (which did not prevent twenty convicts being simultaneously hanged publicly at Newgate); Blue Stocking Clubs were founded; John Philip Kemble took the town by storm on his first appearance as Hamlet at Drury Lane; and that precious scamp, George, Prince of Wales, morganatically married Mrs. Fitzherbert in her drawing-room in Park Lane.

27

CHAPTER II

1786–90

MAIDEN LANE was never of any great length, and hard by the barber's, alongside the still-extant Bedford Head Inn, stood a print-shop and framer's. But its proprietor, John Raphael Smith, was no ordinary tradesman. Not only had his mezzotint-engravings popularised Reynolds, and were to glean him a fortune through reproductions of the work of Morland, but he was himself a miniature painter, a pupil of Pether (musician and mechanic, as well as painter), with an individual style of graceful charm. Hail-fellow-well-met, Smith was a member of the jovial artistic coterie which included Rowlandson, J. R. Cozens, the sensitive, indolent water-colourist, and their patrons, as well as 'Madcap' George Morland, who was at this time twenty-three.

The worthy Smith had, like Stothard and the others, observed and admired the low-priced drawings pinned up round Old Turner's door, and now suggested to the barber that, as his promising lather-boy son was evidently free from schooling, the youth might come along the Lane and colour prints with flat wash at a shilling or two a time.

The barber at first demurred. Billy was doing very well as he was. Apart from making himself useful in the shop, he was studying floral-drawing under Mr. Palice at the Soho Academy, and having occasional tuition from Humphrey Repton, the literary landscape-gardener of Romford. On being pressed, however, the loquacious parent decided that all the various labours might be combined. In these uncertain times, with all the trouble in India, and Warren Hastings even then being impeached for treason, any honest penny turned would help the family budget. When all was said and done, Billy was turned eleven now. A young artist could not begin earning too soon. . . . Had he not already disposed of drawings hung for sale at the door? Besides, who was to tell what might not come out of even such a small beginning?

And so on and so forth. . . . In short, the matter was settled; and in 1786, the year of Frederick the Great's death, Turner the Great settled at the age of eleven his first job, one from which much was indirectly to spring. In a sense, one might say, 1786 was as significant a date for Turner as for Robert Burns, whose first volume of poems was then published.

Contemporaries describe the youthful Turner of this period as being short, sturdy, and untidy, a sailor-like kind of boy, with even features which were large and of a Jewish cast, but with eyes of clear grey-blue. The mouth was as determined as that of someone much older, and the same impression of age was conveyed by his taciturnity and reserve.

Turner was to find, working alongside of him at Raphael Smith's, a young fellow of his own age—only two months older, indeed—who was in every respect his antithesis save in their mutual possession of exceptional artistic talent.

Thomas Girtin, Welsh by birth, and called Honest Tom by all his many friends, was as open and vivacious as Turner was close and tongue-tied. Though Turner subsequently painted Girtin's portrait, the generally-accepted likeness is by W. Opie, and depicts him as dark, keen, frank, hearty, generous, with jutting features, black curling hair, and bold laughing eyes.

Of his ill-fated genius there is ample corroboration even beyond the works of his to be seen at the Victoria & Albert and British Museums, as well as the far larger number in private collections. In later life Turner, who always had the greatest admiration for his friend's abilities, declared that "If Tom Girtin had lived, I should have starved". And it is said that the whole art of Constable (born in 1776, one year later than Girtin and Turner) was transformed by his perusal of thirty drawings by Girtin. They changed him, it is averred, from an amateur to a painter; for it was Girtin's particular quality to bring new generosity of outlook by his sweeping dash and gallant indifference to pettifogging detail.

But the triumphs of Girtin's early-blossoming maturity were yet to come. The work which he and Turner, at eleven years old, sat side by side to do at the back of Raphael Smith's print-shop in Maiden Lane may seem simple, but skill is called for, and trained skill, in the laying evenly of flat washes in

30

pure brown or green or pink tint, such as we see on Gillray prints—some of which, for all we know, may have been coloured by the greater master. A monotonous task, truly, and doubtless more trying to the volatile Girtin than the dogged Turner; but nevertheless not without value as experience in breadth of tone and slickness of brushwork. In later life, when someone commiserated with Turner upon the drudgery of his early labours, he admitted in characteristically manly fashion that Girtin and himself owed much to Smith's training.

"Well!" quoth he, "And what could have been better practice?"

Neither of these Jacks was a dull boy, and their lives were certainly not all play and no work. Neither was of the book-worm type: both were healthy animals, nature-lovers, and fired with ambition regarding its delineation. So all their spare time was spent together in the open air, on walking or boating expeditions, but always on sketching expeditions. The weather never entered into their calculations—nor did it ever, in Turner's case, until the end of his long, full life.

For their country jaunts the boys had not far to go. There were farms and haystacks in Bloomsbury, and the saintly Whitefield was preaching in the meadows where Harley Street now stands. St. Pancras, St. John's Wood and Camden Town were open country, extending on to Hampstead, and farmed by dairymen, one of whom, renting a portion of the Park at Gloucester Gate, was the ancestor of Cecil Rhodes.

One can visualise the keen eyes of the two embryonic geniuses darting eagerly hither and thither, Girtin with the partly-trained outlook of one who had already studied under an Aldersgate Street drawing-master and received tuition from Raphael Smith, Turner with the intensity of imaginative observation and critical summary of detail which was his leading characteristic.

But their chief happy hunting-ground was the Thames, Turner renewing an acquaintanceship happily begun at Brentford, and Girtin, a Southwark boy, born in Great Bandy Leg Walk, introducing his crony to favourite spots on the shelving beaches of West-minster and Lambeth.

At that time those shores were quaint and picturesque. There were still thatched roofs on the tumbledown gabled houses, ramshackle wooden warehouses black with age, fishermen's huts with nets drying on the foreshore, the ruins of John of Gaunt's Palace at the Savoy Steps for both boys to sketch, and grim old wharves leaning out over the waterway—so busy with its clumsy homely rivercraft, dingy barges, wherries, patched sails and spider's-web rigging, moving slowly through the soot and fog. Here Turner must first have envisaged the poetry that lies in ruins: here without question was born his predilection for marine subjects.

His first view of the sea, however, was at Bristol,

32

where he stayed with an old friend of his father, one Narraway, a fellmonger (dealer in skins) in Broadmead. First going there in 1786, when we hear of him setting out sketching on a borrowed pony, he made frequent subsequent visits, and a large number of his drawings executed there are still extant, including boats and shipping with pig-tailed sailormen, many views of Clifton, the likenesses of two of his host's children, and a self-portrait made by request of the Narraway family.

"How am I to do it?" asked the boy.

"In your bedroom, with a looking-glass," was the reply; resulting in a weakly-drawn representation (eventually bequeathed to Ruskin, after Turner's death, by the Master's housekeeper and mistress, Mrs. Danby) of an ingenuous boyish visage framed in long hair curling down on to the shoulders of a frilled jacket.

At this impressionable age—'wax to receive and marble to retain'—the sea was to figure again immediately; for his father decided that his Billy needed further education, and despatched him to an inexpensive school at Margate. Margate, then a charming unsophisticated fishing-village on a broad expanse of sands, was selected, just as the countryside of Brentford had previously been, out of concern for the boy Turner's health; though the reason for such concern is not manifest to the modern biographer, who finds in contemporary accounts invariable reference to Turner as a stocky, seamanlike, weather-proof youth.

Perchance it was merely that the devoted barber was a hen with but one solitary chick; or maybe his motive was to free a beloved son from pernicious and unhappy association with a demented mother.

Though he did not at Mr. Coleman's school at Margate imbibe a smattering of any foreign language, nor even the ability to spell his own, he must there have picked up some rudiments of classical mythology, and been taught enough geography to instil in him the desire to travel, for both figured in his subsequent career. What a pity it is that he did not learn also enough of elementary chemistry to enable him to select and mix colours which did not fade and perish, like those used in much of his greatest work!

Though his schooldays there ended after only a few months, his affection for Margate endured until his deathbed, and was in his thoughts at the last. He returned to the spot many times, and it was there that the great tragedy of his life (the *only* tragedy, in the opinion of the present writer) occurred, one which was to have considerable influence both upon his work and mode of existence. But for the moment it suffices to remember that that first voyage down to Margate—for voyage it must have seemed in those days—took him in a lumbering hoy right through the Pool of London, crowded with colliers, merchantmen, barquentines, and every kind of shipping, past Woolwich Royal Dockyard, where Peter the Great earned his bread as a wheelwright, to Greenwich Hospital, with its knee-breeched pensioners parading, and on

34

to Thanet—all romantic, rich material for that young but so miraculously observant poet's eye.

Meanwhile 'Honest Tom' Girtin, their association temporarily broken, was not to stand idle, with all too few years of life in which to make his deathless name. Though still working as pupil and employee of the agreeable Raphael Smith, there was nevertheless his career to be thought of. The younger of two sons, his father had been killed in the hunting-field when Tom was only three years old. The well-to-do young widow removed from Southwark to St. Martin's-le-Grand, and it is possibly owing to her having then married a pattern-draughtsman named Vaughan that her elder son, John, was apprenticed to an engraver, and Honest Tom, the younger, to Edward Dayes, a perspective draughtsman, who, with a partner, Thomas Malton, conducted a drawing-school at Malton's lodgings in Long Acre.

Dayes was not without talent—critics still speak reservedly of his neat, careful studies with small figures, and dry manner—but there is conclusive evidence that he was jealous of, and even spiteful towards, his more promising pupils and apprentices, Girtin included. By the time, however, that Turner's schooling at Margate was completed, Girtin's kicking against the Dayes pricks had not materialised, and Old Turner, always affectionately anxious for his son's advancement, and doubtless stimulated by Girtin's successful example, arranged that Billy should become a pupil of Dayes' partner, Malton, a fellow

35

as forthright and irascible as Dayes was cold, exacting
and precise.

In later years, Turner, with the unique generosity
of an artist, declared: "My real master was Tom
Malton, of Long Acre." The detached critic might
venture to say that the tribute, if not strictly true,
was equally not merely complimentary, since perspective figures somewhat importantly both in Turner's
art and career. But the crass historical truth is that
Malton discarded Turner as impenetrably dull, to the
great mortification of Turner's father. In the wheel
of Time's revenges, however, came the equally indisputable fact that the despised pupil was to be appointed
Professor of Perspective at the Royal Academy, a position
to which the impatient Malton could never have aspired.

Honest Tom now quarrelled with Malton's partner,
Edward Dayes. It may or may not have been owing
to the rejection of Turner by Malton, but I like to
think that in those days, if not in these, loyal friendship did exist. Tom's complaint was that Dayes
deliberately gave him servile and inartistic work to
do, and on these grounds he refused to be bound by
the words, instead of the spirit, of his apprenticeship.

The years have shown that Girtin had genius, and
have not shown that Dayes had, so we must withhold
our judgment when recording that Dayes not only
refused to cancel Girtin's indentures, but obtained a
legal Order whereby Honest Tom was imprisoned in
Bridewell as a refractory apprentice. What Turner
would have done in the like circumstances gives

pleasant rein to fancy; but the indomitable Girtin softened his incarceration by making drawings on the walls of his cell.

In those brutal times, and for a considerable period yet to come, privileged persons were allowed to view convicted persons as if they were animals in a menagerie. (One recalls Dickens and Macready recognising with horror their former friend, Thomas Griffiths Wainewright, poet, painter, and poisoner, in a felon's cell.) It happened with lucky Girtin, however, that one such visitor to Bridewell was the Earl of Essex, who, attracted by the prisoner's drawings, and hearing his story from the turnkey, purchased the artist's indentures, burnt them before his eyes, obtained his freedom, and became his patron, taking him to work in the luxury of his Cassiobury estate, as an antidote to prison, and subsequently securing his admission to the Royal Academy Schools.

The doors which opened so magically, then and thereafter, to Girtin's charm, were not for the likes of Turner, dour and self-contained. Still working for Raphael Smith in tinting prints (to which labour Girtin also in due course returned) he was put to study at the School of Art in St. Martin's Lane conducted by Paul Sandby, one of the foundation members of the Royal Academy. The hairdresser may have been ignorant and tight-fisted, but common fairness compels one to admit that he invariably had the generosity to give his son every opportunity permitted by his meagre and hard-earned income.

37

It was Sandby, 'the father of water-colour', who first taught Turner to paint in that exquisite medium ('a toy for young ladies, or an instrument in the hands of a master') in which he was later so sublimely to excel. Though then, as now, to the auctioneer-mind water-colours were mere 'drawings', in contradistinction to real paintings—viz: those in which oil-pigments have been used. There had begun to be an increasing demand, in those days before photography, for topographical drawings in colour. Sandby and Richard Wilson, his contemporary, were pioneers in bringing landscapes to the notice of the public by travelling about the provinces picturising historical buildings and landed-proprietors' estates. For a good many years to come Turner was in like fashion to earn the greater part of his living. Not only in this respect was he indebted to Sandby, but also as regards the latter's artistic influence and robust example, clearly discernible in the pupil's early work—as, indeed, is the influence of Malton also, while traces of Wilson's example remain discernible for some time to come. A colour drawing in Sandby's manner, signed *W. Turner*, was purchased in 1788 from the barber's window. We may infer that *W. Turner's* stock had risen in his father's estimation, since the youthful prodigy's jejune efforts no longer had to flutter outside the shop door. We also learn that the minimum prices had soared to two or even three shillings apiece instead of one.

The particular drawing above-mentioned has not

come down to posterity, but the National Gallery has a clumsy sketch, *Nuneham Courtenay*, dated 1787, which shows little of the promise apparent in his first generally-accepted work, *Wanstead Old Church*, painted in water-colour when he was thirteen, in 1788, the year which saw the birth of The Times, the first shipload of convicts to Australia, and the deaths of Bonnie Prince Charlie, Gainsborough, and Charles Wesley. In this year also, George III, never mentally too sound, became definitely insane, stopping his horse in Windsor Park in order to shake hands with the branch of an oak, believing it to be the King of Prussia.

It was a great piece of luck that all Turner's initial training was under masters in perspective, architecture, and landscape. He was not sent to these tutors through any thought-out plan. They happened to be the folk associated with pictorial art who passed across the elder Turner's narrow horizon. Had their specialities been portraits, or subject-pictures, or animal studies, or stained glass, or religious frescoes, the student's youthful fancy might have turned to branches of art other than the land- and sea-scape where lay his especial gift. He could never have been anything but a great master, but at least he would have had to wait much longer for recognition. For just when he 'commenced painter', the connoisseurs, prepared by the work of Claude, and Cuyp, and Salvator Rosa, were ripe to welcome a landscape-artist who should transcend them all.

All the very early works of Turner were done in
his ill-lit attic-bedroom in the small and poky 'upper-
part' in Maiden Lane, where also he—throughout his
long life a glutton for work—spent laborious hours,
when not employed by Raphael Smith, in colouring
designs and washing-in backgrounds for architects.

The dark little house must clearly have consisted of
the living-room in the basement-kitchen, the shop on
the ground-floor, a first-floor bedroom for the barber
(and wife, in her lucid intervals), and the garret where
the young artist slept and worked, the dormer-window
of which overlooked busy, noisy Maiden Lane. Passing
through the entrance in Hand Court, one must have
faced two doors, one half-glazed, leading into the
shop, and a shut one, marked Private, admitting to
the steep and narrow stairs. Behind the perruquier's
saloon must have been another entry to these same
stairs, out of a passage giving access also to the cellar-
kitchen. In the hairdressing trade there is a perpetual
need of hot water, which, in that primitive epoch,
the kitchen-range must have supplied.

Turner's constitutional secretiveness and love of
solitude had already begun to manifest themselves.
Inside his attic, with the warped door closed behind
him, his oak was sported, and all visitors were unwelcome. Even his father was not allowed to see his
work till completed. Hardwick, an architect who
paid him to wash in skies and backgrounds, tell us
'he would never suffer me to see him draw, but
concealed all that he did in his bedroom'.

And a publisher-client, Mr. Britton, records that once, when he made his way unannounced to the garret-workroom, Turner angrily snatched up his work and snapped out: "You shan't see 'em! And mind that next time you come through the shop and not up the back way!"

Corroborative anecdotes have come down to us showing his increasing originality of outlook, and indicating that he already had the courage of his own convictions.

For example, another architect, a Mr. Dobson, complained that in the perspective front of a house which Turner had been given to colour, for a guinea, the youth had sketched realistic windows, with glass reflecting light, instead of washing in the traditional flat slate-coloured panes.

"It must be done as heretofore," declared Dobson.

"It will spoil my drawing," Turner demurred.

But the architect insisted, so Turner, thrifty by heredity, had unwillingly to obey. But he would never afterwards accept employment from the same source.

Commissions from other architects were not hard to come by. Porden, who designed for the Prince-Regent-to-be that preposterous Pavilion at Brighton, was so enamoured of the young Turner's designs (viewed, I like to imagine, while having his love-locks tended by the pushful and log-rolling barber) that he offered to take the promising youth as an apprentice without premium.

The opening was rejected. Doubtless the sturdily independent Billy had something to say; though when, just later, the barber came into an unexpected windfall of £200, his son raised no objection to the money being used for the purchase of indentures with Hardwick, the architect with whom he had been amicably working for some time past.

It is difficult to read without impatience the many accounts of Turner Senior, which disparage him as mean and money-grubbing. No one who has not been the father of growing sons can know how extraordinarily hard it is for a parent to sink his still-vital personality in the selfless propagation of his progeny's advancement. For such abnegation to be appreciated is rare in any epoch, but the Maiden Lane barber fully deserved the almost unique filial affection which helped to make the younger Turner's life a poem. What we with certainty know about this father is that in his unlettered ignorance he had the imagination to foresee his son's pre-eminence: in his provincial niggardliness he had the generosity to spend his all upon his son's tuition. He taught him the dignity and power of work and thrift: he showed him love and loyalty transcending woman's: he not only brought genius into being, but nurtured it to the full extent of his humble powers. Good sons are rarer than good fathers, but here for once were both.

William Turner did not lose his £200. Hardwick, after a period of trial, considered Billy unsuited—or, maybe, wasted—as an architect, and with a nicety of conscience surely as rare in his profession as in others, returned the money in full. He suggested that the youth should discard compass and T-square for palette and brush, and study painting at the Royal Academy Schools, where Tom Girtin was already installed. His obviously disinterested advice was taken. Turner was now fourteen; the year was 1789, and the anxiety in Maiden Lane during his period of probation at Somerset House doubtless far outweighed any concern felt in the family circle regarding the storming of the Bastille and the mutiny on the 'Bounty' both of which took place just then, or interest either in the publication of Blake's "Songs of Innocence," or in the fact that the United States had just elected their first President in the person of one George Washington.

Hardwick remained on the friendliest terms with the barber and his son. When, long afterwards, the architect (who always firmly disclaimed any share in Turner's subsequent success) mischievously showed J. M. W. some of his immature early efforts, the artist remembered them perfectly, and, in reference to a view of Lambeth, said:

"Ha! Yes: up against that inn there was a board stuck up, on which was written—'Be Sober. Be Vigilant'; and close by were the parish stocks, I remember."

The Academy Schools did not at that period teach landscape-painting (and according to Ruskin taught Turner nothing) but there at least the young artist

43

for the first time drew from the antique and the nude. Studies, in the quaintly-named Plaster Academy, from the plaster-cast, classical and anatomical, occupied him till the end of 1791. And during the following year or so he signed in as attending the life-class forty-eight times. Which brings us to one of the most prevalent legends regarding Turner (retailed in due course to the present author when an art-student) —that he could not draw the figure. It is true that only too often he did not trouble to do so, as if it were unworthy of attention in comparison with elemental Nature, and he certainly almost always subordinated any figures to the main theme of his subjects. But apart from the numberless proofs, in his sketch-books at the National Gallery, and the many completed works which testify his ability when he so chose, *Venus and Adonis*, for example, the lightly-indicated personages—and animals—in some of his major works are undeniably masterly in suggestion.

We art-students were likewise informed that a large quantity of brilliant figure-studies in the sketch-books had been suppressed by Victorian-minded Ruskin on the score of their indecency, like a quantity of splendid Rowlandsons I have myself inspected, but, unfortunately, 'what the soldier said is not evidence'.

It may, however, interest carpers to learn that for quite a while Turner was a protégé of Sir Joshua Reynolds, in whose house in Leicester Fields he copied portraits, and that but for the tragic blindness and subsequent death of the elder artist in 1792, our

genius might easily have become and remained a
portrait-painter—I had almost said, *only* a portrait-
painter. His self-likeness in the early twenties, now
in the National Gallery, awakens exciting speculation
as to the outcome. The elder Ruskin found, on
Turner's death, a number of portraits 'in various
styles' from his brush, but neither originals nor
reproductions are available for scrutiny.

This was the time when, Turner being present at
a lecture of Sir Joshua's in the great hall of Somerset
House, the floor gave way. After the panic had
subsided, Reynolds, who had remained serene,
remarked: "If we had all perished, the Art of England
would have been set back five hundred years." He
spoke indeed more truly than he knew.

There are comparatively little other data available
of Turner as an R.A. student. He drew *The Genius
of the Vatican* there, and became friends with Henry
Aston Barker and Robert (afterwards Sir Robert)
Ker Porter, as well as Girtin. Into the lives of Girtin
and himself was now to come a new and salutary
influence. The debonair Raphael Smith, in whose
back room the youths continued to turn an honest
penny, had for client and crony a certain Dr. Thomas
Monro, one of the mental specialists attending poor
George III. The worthy physician, a patron of the
arts in a fashion unhappily extinct, invited the two
clever lads to his hospitable fireside, next door to
David Garrick's, in Adelphi Terrace, where every
evening similarly promising students were made

welcome to copy pictures in his valuable collection, partake of oyster-suppers, earn a shilling or two in pocket-money, and receive free medical advice when needed.

The *chefs d'œuvre* which hung round the good Doctor's walls and swelled his innumerable portfolios gave the two aspirants their first glimpses of Old and Modern Masters upon which their maturer work was modelled—notably Canaletto in the case of Girtin; and, for Turner, Vandervelde, Wilson, and de Loutherbourg, R.A., the Polish nobleman, who had formerly painted scenery at Drury Lane for Garrick. It was apropos a marine-subject by Vandervelde that Turner said with emotion in later years: "Ah! that made me a painter!"

At the Doctor's house, a rallying-point for promising artists of the day, the lads came into personal contact with Cotman, Varley, and John Robert Cozens, an already successful water-colourist of the utmost delicacy and sensibility, specialising in those atmospheric effects which Turner, admittedly inspired by him, first imitated and then surpassed. Poor Cozens, who, according to Fuseli, 'drew with an enchanted hand', was a patient of Dr. Monro's as well as a friend, and died early in a madhouse. He only exhibited once in the Royal Academy, a Hannibal study, upon which Turner frankly founded his own subsequent treatment of the subject.

Two doors away in Adelphi Terrace lived John Henderson, another art-collector and connoisseur, where the boys also visited and sketched during the winter evenings. This gentleman later presented to the British Museum a collection of the work of both young artists.

In summer they frequently walked out to Dr. Monro's country house in Hertfordshire.

"There!" said Turner once, pointing towards Harrow, "Girtin and I have often walked to Bushey and back to make drawings for good Dr. Monro at half a crown apiece and a supper."

One is entitled to consider, however, that, even in the economical Turner's case, and certainly in the dashing Girtin's, it was not solely the half-crown and supper that attracted them, but the opportunity to study at first hand, intimately, and at their leisure, originals by such masters as Rembrandt, Claude, Richard Wilson, Snyders, Paul Potter, Salvator Rosa, and Ostade.

In 1790, when Turner was fifteen, Boswell's "Life of Johnson" saw the light, Adam ("Wealth of Nations") Smith died, and Turner exhibited for the first time in the Royal Academy—a 14 x 10 water-colour *View of the Archbishop's Palace, Lambeth.*

CHAPTER III

1791–1802

PAPA TURNER always encouraged his Billy's
sketching trips, despite the outlay in journey-money
and for meals which could be obtained more ec-
onomically at home. And the young artist's excursions
to Kent, and particularly to Margate, became surprisingly frequent for a temperament so shut-in and
ungregarious that its owner was able to make a world
of his own wherever there was a closed door, a table,
a chair or upturned box, paper, ink, pens, charcoal,
dry bread for erasure, and privacy.

His output of the period leaves no doubt that the
Medway had a particular attraction for him; his first
drawing to be engraved was of Rochester, and the
whole county had for him an enduring appeal. Just
as so many otherwise-conventional Englishwomen like
to imagine, indeed to boast, that they have in their
blood some picturesque and interesting foreign strain
—French, Spanish, or Italian: even Jewish—so, as
the chalk cliffs and hopfields of Kent were romantic
to the femininely-primitive Turner, he was wont
throughout his life to hint that he had Kentish origins.
There was no shadow of justification for this amiable
weakness; it is undeniable that his father hailed from
Devonshire, his mother from Nottingham, via Isling-

48

ton, and that he himself was born just off the Strand.
The agreeable tarrydiddle is on a par with that other
illusion of his middle-age that he was born in the
same year as Napoleon.

In the case of Kent it was, to be indulgent, under-
standable. It was at Margate that he first saw the
sea, his devotion for which was so steadfast that he
may justly be said to have interpreted and revealed it
to thousands, painters as well as public, who would
otherwise have merely thought of it as wet, and salt,
and a concomitant of bathing huts. It was at Margate
also that he fell in love.

Even in our own hectic, complex period, where
falling in love and out again does not cease with
marriage or maturity, first-love still has a beauty
never afterwards recaptured. The possibility, to-day,
that one's first love could also be one's last love is so
rare, so improbable save in the romantic fiction of
the cinema-screen, that it merely excites derision.
Nevertheless, because it throws light on much which
is otherwise unexplainable, it is my purpose to persuade you that, in the case of Turner, it was precisely
that unlikely thing which happened.

One must remember, to begin with, that his age
was not our age: it was incredibly more simple-
minded, more single-minded. What proportion of
Englishmen and -women nowadays truly worship God,
undoubtingly credit the divinity of Christ? Not one
in a thousand: excluding 'those who go down to the
sea in ships', since faith in Something is all one has

to cling to when at the mercy of the elements. Yet in those days the vast majority believed sincerely, not as cant, in lip-worship, or for graft. You may say that the march of science has educated us: perhaps it has taught us better about love also. But Turner, recollect, had not the mixed blessing of our dubious culture.

There is, moreover, Turner's own character to take into account. Taciturn, shut-in, unread, uncouth, he was already at fifteen sufficient unto himself, not at all the sort of youth to consult or confide in either his father or his only friend, the flippant, devil-may-care Tom Girtin. Add to which that he was a visionary, inspired, a poetic genius as yet unable to express himself, beneath the clumsy exterior of a fisher-lad. Can one be surprised that when he fell in love, with the precocity contemporaneously revealed in his work, it was a mortal wound?

There are all too little authenticated data of the attachment. She was the sister of one of his school-fellows at the Margate Seminary, whom he met again by chance on one of his subsequent visits to the district. She was about the same age as he, and the attraction was mutual; but it was, of course, a boy and girl affair, and naturally smiled upon as calf-love by their elders. In Turner's mind, however, it is clear, was embedded from the very first the certainty that this was the real thing, the one and only romance of his existence. Conscious of his own potentialities, he was confident that it was only a question of time before he had something worth offering the loved one. And, with an object to be worked for, he applied himself even more doggedly than before to earning money, and to a henceforward-etherealised Art.

When Turner left Margate, after his avowal, leaving the young girl a self-portrait, it is certain he considered himself unconditionally affianced. And we have no proof that there was any reservation or apathy on the part of his betrothed. But I think it may fairly be advanced on her behalf that she had no possible means of knowing that the tongue-tied, shy, sentimental, somewhat undersized, untidy boy to whom she had lost her untutored heart was destined to be the great man he knew he had it in him to become. While in the loved one's presence, she, like all of us, would ignore irrelevant materialistic details like careers, and ways and means. But suppose months passed without a sight or word of him, would she not be justified in wondering whether his blurted, ill-phrased vows were serious, sincere? And when one gets to know Turner the man, as I claim to have done, it is impossible to blindfold oneself to the likelihood of his having left Margate confident that she thought exactly as he did—that the matter was settled—it only needed his carving of a career, his making a living, to complete their happiness—and that, under such circumstances, what difference could trivial things like letters make? There, I maintain, comes the rub. Turner was illiterate; he was primarily and fanatically a worker; he was shortly—with the object of making money

51

quickly—to be extremely busy and much away from home: he, cautious as ever, may, even in those days before the Penny Post, have considered the franking of letters an unnecessary expense: but, whatever the complicated motive, I feel as certain as if the man had told me so himself that Turner let months go by without a line to the disappointed and decreasingly-affectionate girl, in the sublime belief that her mind was as immutable as was his own when set on any object.

Previous biographers talk of a malevolent step-mother, but this I unhesitatingly reject as fiction. The young lady cannot have lacked beauty, or Turner's all-seeing eye would not have selected her as an ideal: and there were doubtless personable young fellows in the village of Margate who also had eyes and lips. I commiserate with Turner deeply in what I have already referred to as the one real tragedy of his life, but I cannot in equity allow all the blame to be assigned to his inamorata or any fairy step-mother.

Let me not give the impression that there was any immediate swift finality to the occurrence which was to sour Turner's mental outlook—or dignify and enlarge it, according to the point of view. Much Medway water was to flow under Kentish bridges before the culmination which certainly caused Turner to remain a bachelor, but not, as I shall show, a lonely one.

From Girtin's *Rochester* drawing, dated 1791, we may reasonably infer that Honest Tom accompanied Turner on one of his incursions to Kent. In the same year Mozart died, and George, Prince of Wales, was warned off the Turf for running his race-horse Escape 'on the cross' at Newmarket.

Shortly afterwards Girtin found a new patron, James Moore, with whom he was to be associated for some years. Moore's father, a wholesale linen draper in Cheapside, had been a neighbour of the Girtin family in Southwark. The son, succeeding to the business, conceived an enthusiasm for antiquities, and dispersed the profits of the Cheapside store in scouring the provinces for materials for his *magnum opus*, "Monastic Remains and Ancient Castles in England and Wales." Girtin was employed to make completed drawings from Moore's rough drafts, and on occasion to supply views of his own. The aspiring tradesman seems to have been not over-generous, either in acknowledgment of his assistant's participation, or in respect of payment, seeing that all Girtin got was six shillings for a whole day's work, or three when his services were needed for the half-day only.

The association is emphasised because it quite evidently gave Turner the notion of doing likewise. In 1792 he secured orders from Walker, the engraver and publisher of The Copper Plate Magazine to make a series of topographical drawings. This commission took Turner on the first of his many provincial sketching tours, where his earlier grounding in perspective by Malton, and in architecture by Hardwick, was to prove such value, and to which posterity is indebted for his vast range of theme. With a capacity for tireless industry almost superhuman, he travelled the country principally on foot, thinking nothing of twenty and thirty miles a day, in addition to his commissioned labours. We learn of a draughtsman-companion who was walked off his feet, and fell out by the wayside, glad to let Turner continue on his own sweet way, which consisted of making sketches as he walked, and re-touching them while munching his frugal meals by the roadside, sleeping on haystacks or hard tap-room benches. And all the time filling his brain and notebooks with impressions which his observant eye, level head, retentive memory and poet's vision told him might be useful later.

At the end of this first extended tour, just about the time that Louis XVI's head fell into the basket of the guillotine, Turner was sufficiently encouraged by further commissions, notably from Harrison for his Pocket Magazine, to feel justified in renting a proper studio for himself in Hand Court. He still slept above the barber's, and so kept in close touch with his father, but the premises, besides being obviously more convenient for his work, were less noisy than Maiden Lane itself, though actually somewhat darker.

One unforeseen disadvantage was that unwelcome visitors could not so easily be sidetracked. About 1793, a pertinacious dealer penetrated to the new studio, with an offer to buy other work. Turner was never one to refuse good money, nor, once he was launched as a professional artist, did he err in putting too low a cash value on his work. On this occasion the middleman jibbed at the price demanded. Chaffer as he might, however, he could not get it lowered.

"I have a better picture below that cost less," he at last declared.

"Oh, you have—have you?" grunted Turner, sceptically.

"Yes, I have—in a fly at the door."

"If that's so," returned the artist, "it must be one of Tom Girtin's."

The generous tribute was on a par with another remark he made to Girtin himself, on seeing a drawing by the latter of St. Paul's.

"No man living could do this but you," he insisted.

The close friendship between the two young painters still continued, though their paths had begun to lie in different directions. Turner, whose strange duplicate existence as visionary and materialist had already begun, was setting himself to give his market what it wanted. He even first experimented in oil upon realising that only in that medium could he expect tangible recognition from the hide-bound panjandrums of the Academy.

Girtin, on the other hand, though he exhibited at the R.A. four years after Turner, and continued to do so yearly until his early death, remained until 1801 exclusively a water-colour man, looking to private collectors for his market. His manly beauty and great personal attraction, apart from his exquisite art, gained him generous and devoted admirers wherever he went.

In 1793–4 we find him with James Moore at Ely, by this time 'bettering', we learn, 'the instruction of his masters', while Turner was away in Wales and the Western Counties sketching for his engraver-employers. Later we hear of them together at Dover, with Turner making painstaking studies of the shipping, accompanied by Mr. Henderson, good Dr. Monro's neighbour in Adelphi Terrace.

Among a number of Cathedrals and Abbeys depicted about this time by Turner are Peterborough, Lincoln, Shrewsbury, Canterbury, and Malvern. The last-named returned from the Academy unsold, and had to be bartered with the frame-maker for his bill. And disbelievers in his ability to portray the human figure will please note that in this year and the next he exhibited two domestic interiors, one of children playing by a cottage fire, another of a labourer's wife bending over her cooking-utensils. We also learn that in his growing love of colour he would irrelevantly introduce into his studies a rainbow or a peacock.

The extent of his output at this period is barely credible. Though in the next four years he was to contribute no less than thirty-nine subjects to the Academy, he now for the first time took up etching, in which he shortly so excelled that in this branch of art alone he would have made a reputation sufficient for any other man's ambition.

But these flights into foreign fields (mainly, one

may surmise, for prestige) in no way stemmed the flood of his topographical and architectural bread-and-butter work. Prior to this state in his career, it may fairly be said that he was inclined to be satisfied in basing his style and even subject-matter on that of brother-craftsmen; just as the itch to emulate and outdo his professional rivals in their own chosen sphere did not leave him until late middle-life. Even though this imitative tendency may have sprung from ingrained caution, it was clearly also partly due to his frenzy for isolation, resulting in his having to puzzle out for himself technical problems much more easily solved through verbal hints from others and visual example of their working-methods. He might, indeed, just as well have studied on a desert island as at Hand Court. Now, however, his natural diffidence being overcome by the security bred of orders pouring in, he first revealed an individuality of outlook and technique. Before Paul Sandby, water-colour painting was little more than tinting: Turner perfected where the earlier pioneer experimented: so that the two of them, teacher and pupil, have indisputable claim to be creators of the Art as it is to-day. Moreover, to the younger man's concentration upon, and mastery of, this medium, may be assigned his success in oils as a landscape-painter, where so many of his predecessors never fulfilled their early promise.

1795 is ear-marked in English History as the year when 'The First Gentleman in Europe' was drunk at his state wedding with the Princess Caroline of Brunswick, whom he brutishly discarded after the birth of her daughter, Charlotte, in the following year. In 1795 we hear, also, of Mme. de Stael at Mickleham, where she headed the colony of French émigrés. Turner was now twenty and we find him and his easel, under a big 'gamp' umbrella, stranded in a punt on a mudbank some distance from the shore, his concentration on his work being such that he had not noticed the ebbing of the tide. We hear that he could tour and live for five days on a guinea, but that, still unsatisfied with his earning-power, he found a quicker method of turning out work of equal quality, by adopting a broader, simpler style. Also, as if not having labours enough, he started giving lessons, not only in London, but at Hadley and elsewhere, first at five shillings, then ten, and finally at a guinea, per hour. The enterprise cannot be counted as one of his successes. Always reticent, and unused to mixing in any kind of society, he was quite unable to express his criticisms, and his tuition was solely by ocular demonstration. His pupils complained that he was impatient, brusque and rude; and one of them, William Blake, already an artist of great distinction, twenty years older than the youthful tutor, declares he was left quite alone. For the first time, however, we hear of Turner's caustic humour; and at least one pleasing anecdote has come down to us from an experiment soon ended.

It appears that a pupil who had missed her

lesson came to the next one volubly full of excuses and apologies.

"All very well, ma'am," interrupted Turner, holding out his hand. "But—one guinea, if you please."

We have seen our young hero slaving hectically to establish himself in his profession to justify himself in thinking of immediate marriage, though still not of age; and the whole of his history goes to show that he was never the fellow to take responsibility lightly, that on the contrary he smeared his personal legend by his constitutional reluctance, anxiety, and suspicion in all money-matters. How final a proof of love was it in his case, therefore, that in 1796 he went joyfully to Margate and laid his all at his lady's feet. How infinitely more devastating than in the case of another must have come the discovery that the loved one had, not so much been unfaithful, as had exercised her woman's prerogative to find someone else she preferred. Worse, the marriage was to take place immediately— and here, to my mind, is corroboration that Turner, in his unworldly romanticism and impervious concentration of purpose, had taken the girl far too much for granted, had heedlessly neglected her. Surely, otherwise, he would have known what was afoot, what did in fact occur within a week of his getting the shock of the news? When we learn that in his futile protests and appeals he stormed and raged—he, the monosyllabic, walled-in with restraint—we get some glimpse of that chaotic upheaval in his tortured soul which was to make him avoid all womankind for many

59

a year, and never view them in the light of marriage, develop distrust till it became a mania, shut out friendship, and drive him into the prison of his own strange nature, from which he was only able eventually to emerge through the pursuit of parallel identities. If Robert Louis Stevenson, born before Turner died, did not conceive the first notion of "Dr. Jekyll and Mr. Hyde" with Turner in his mind, he might easily have done so, for that fiction is rendered credible by Turner's life, after his abortive, thwarted love-affair.

The immediate result was that the wounded, lonely, hope-bereft creature hid himself in his work even more closely than before. One may imagine that his concerned father, apprehending much that was unspoken, would endeavour to deflect the son's low spirits with light chatter of the hairdresser's saloon— how that poor dear witty Mr. Horace Walpole had passed on, as well as another of his customers, Macklin, the actor, whose faculties had left him while in the act of playing Shylock, so that they had difficulty in getting him from the theatre to his lodgings in Tavistock Court, Covent Garden. God rest both their souls! And as to how he himself had fulfilled a splendid order, supplying all the wigs for that classic-to-be, "The Heir-at-Law," just successfully produced by George Colman the Younger. And all the other gossip of the town. . . .

But it was of no avail. Turner, impulsive, irritable, ardent, sensitive, was full of a strange pride born of the consciousness that against all evidence he was one of the great ones of the earth. Impatient even of sympathy, he sought to forget his tragedy in travel, and set out on a sketching-tour in Yorkshire, Cumberland, and Durham. His artists' materials formed the greater part of his impedimenta, since we learn that, apart from his ungainly umbrella, his personal luggage was enclosed in a handkerchief. We hear also for the first time of his flute, so inappropriately characteristic. Throughout his early manhood and right into middle-age he was wont to amuse himself by practising on it whenever there was no longer any light to paint by. It, and music for it, went with him on all his sketching-trips, and even on this Northern Tour may have earned him free suppers in the pot-houses of his choice. On foot, on pony-back, and occasionally by stage-coach, his abounding energy swiftly covers the country, the thick-set, bandy-legged, eager-eyed, indomitable mystic. For the stage of mere topographical drawings is over: he is a student and a servant no longer: henceforward the embittered adult is to rely upon himself alone, and follow his poetic star.

The trip was not only lucrative, but brought other fruitful results by bringing him into touch with Dr. Whittaker, the historian, with whom he was afterwards to be associated in the "History of Richmondshire," with his future patrons, Lord Harewood, and Sir John Leicester, who subsequently became Lord de Tabley, and above all with Mr. Walter Fawkes, the Squire of Farnley Hall, Otley, near Harrogate, who was to succeed Girtin as his greatest friend. His outlook

upon Yorkshire at this tragic time, moreover, gave
its scenery, the first of its kind he had encountered, a
romantic aspect, so that that county held henceforward
first place in his affections—to such an extent that some
critics profess to find more of Yorkshire than of
Switzerland in his pictures of the Alps painted a year
or two later.

This is the period when Nelson won the Battle of
the Nile, Coleridge's "Ancient Mariner" appeared, and
more public dismay was caused by Pitt's introduction
of Income Tax, starting at 2*d*. in the £, than in the
well-nigh-unprintable atrocities of the Irish Rebellion.
The same date brought Turner's National Gallery
self-portrait, previously referred to. Unremarkable in
colour, even indeed as art, the features are naturally
of interest, and we already find indications of the
afterwards unduly prominent nose, full lower lip, and
slightly staring, glassy-blue eyes which were to give
Count D'Orsay, and others, material for caricature.
The picture, unlike much of Turner's work, remains
in perfect preservation, probably due to the fact that it
was painted under Academy supervision, with pigments
supplied which were orthodox and non-experimental.

This was one of his first known works in oil, though
we hear also at this date of his using that medium for
sketches of Rochester and of a sunset at Battersea.
His first oil-painting to be hung in the Academy, in
1797, was a moonlight study of Millbank, rendered
trebly interesting, in the light of subsequent history,
from the facts that he was fated to die not far from

the scene, near Cremorne Pier, and that, still later on, it was at Millbank, in the Tate Gallery, that so many of his masterpieces were to rest. Ruskin speaks of his style at this period as 'stern in manner, reserved, quiet, grave in colour, forceful in hand!' And an actual contemporary, speaking of *Fishermen* in this year, says: 'Particularly struck with a sea-view by Turner . . . bold in design and masterly in execution. I am entirely unacquainted with the artist; but if he proceeds as he has begun, he cannot fail to become the first in his department.'

Immediately before his being, at twenty-four, elected A.R.A., the Annual Exhibition Catalogue printed the first of those poetical quotations which he was afterwards to delight to add to his pictures. That in 1798 was from Milton, and is significant as indicating the new tendency of his subjects:

' Ye mists and exhalations that now rise
    From hill or steaming lake, dusky or grey
    Till the sun paints your fleecy skirts with gold
    In honour of the world's great author rise.'

The same year he quotes from Thomson's "Seasons", and in 1799 no less than thirty-seven lines from various writers. The inevitable deduction, taking into account Turner's lack of education and known indifference to all the arts not entering his immediate purview, is that he, when lonely and withdrawn into himself after his unhappy love-affair, took to reading . . . just as so many of us have done in kindred circumstances. From this time onwards it is certain that his own poetic visions were intensified and enflamed by the more romantic passages of contemporary writers.

Scott and Byron, who were to influence him to the extent of his attempting himself to write a poetic epic, were still only aspirants to fame; but the age was rich in literary genius, and writers of talent found publishers and patrons where nowadays they would starve, submerged in the spate of pretentious ephemeralia. Burns and Cowper, the one just dead, the other dying, had each completed his life-work, as indeed had Sheridan in respect of drama; Isaac D'Israeli had issued the first two volumes of his "Curiosities of Literature", Blake and Wordsworth were in their prime, Charles Lamb was commencing his career by writing verse, as was Walter Savage Landor; and among the poets living at that date who had already reputations, were the pious Southey, "Ye Mariners of England" Campbell, and Thomas Moore.

There are signs that Turner now began to be discontented with his rates of payment and conditions of work. For each of his nine annual illustrations to The Oxford Almanac he received ten guineas as against the hundred-and-fifty going to the engraver, James Basire. That he was restive under such treatment is shown by his refusing, in the "Parish of Whalley", a book he shortly afterwards illustrated for the Rev. Dr. Whittaker, the archaeologist, to copy a painting he despised instead of supplying an original work. Moreover, according to an arbitrator appointed by the Doctor, he 'wrote very tragically on the subject'. The commentator adds that he despaired of any effective compromise, 'as Turner has all the irritability of youthful genius'.

Turner, of course, won; and we get from the account an impression that he had begun not only to be able to get his own way, but also command his own price. He also commenced refusing to sell a drawing at an agreed price, unless the purchaser likewise took various unwished-for others for an equivalent sum apiece. Such hints are needed to account for the enormous fortune he was able to acquire. Further substantial amounts must also now have come his way through his association with the eccentric William Beckford, author of the English classic "Vathek," written originally in French at a single sitting of two days and three nights. In the story occurs a tower three hundred feet high, containing seven thousand steps, and when Beckford, 'Britain's wealthiest son', succeeded to one million pounds sterling, he conceived the strange idea of transforming the family seat at Fonthill, Wilts., which dated back to the Norman Conquest, and upon the rebuilding of which £240,000 had already been spent, into a replica of the tower in his romance.

The Gothic Abbey, as it was called, was reconstructed by gangs of labourers working day and night in relays without cessation, and Turner, brought there on commission, made a series of paintings of the progress of the work by moonlight, torchlight, sunrise, sunset, and full moon, which were exhibited in the

Academy of 1800. The new Abbey, too hastily erected at the cost of a quarter of a million, subsided to the ground upon completion, when the extraordinary Beckford spent a further £273,000 upon its immediate re-erection. One is inevitably reminded of the Tower of Babel when one learns that, funds getting short, it had to be sold to a stranger, who got little satisfaction from his bargain, since it was not long before the white elephant fell in ruins to the ground once more.

But, in the midst of all this reckless extravagance, we can be sure that Turner took care to have his fair share. It was certainly now that he removed to Harley Street, a district with which he was to be connected for the rest of his life. It is possible, of course, that mental association of his romance with the studio in Hand Court had sickened him of the place. This house in Harley Street, No. 64, he subsequently purchased, together with the one next door, as a speculation, and they represent two out of the three buildings which he owned at death. His father, however, still continued for some years to live over the shop in Maiden Lane.

Turner's removal to a comparatively fashionable portion of the town (though these first premises of his in Harley Street would seem to have been merely a studio and adjoining rooms, not the whole house) seems to have been dictated solely by considerations of space for his work and his increasing craving for seclusion. It in no way altered the mode of life, the squalid, hole-and-corner mode of life, to which he had been bred and was accustomed. We shall later penetrate to 'domestic interiors', almost incredible in their primitive discomfort, but they were the environment this man of genius preferred, and who are we pygmies to say him nay?

How fortunate for the world and for Art it is that Turner was not born a gentleman! In those days the only association the well-bred might have with pictorial art was as patrons and collectors. Byron, an aristocrat before he was an author, wrote just then: 'I know nothing of painting, and I detest it . . . I never was so disgusted in my life as with Rubens . . . and in Spain I did not think much of Murillo and Velasquez. Depend upon it, of all the arts it is the most artificial and unnatural. . . . ' That his noble scorn was in the mode is shown in the high-bred and hybrid memoirs of the age. Had Turner been born the son of one of George III's Court Chamberlains his inspiration would have been forcibly smothered at birth. As it was, he had to fight to gain recognition, a stimulus to all true artist-natures, and one which has nurtured in the stony ground of unappreciative Britain some of the finest painters, novelists, dramatists, poets, essayists and actors that have ever lived.

And, in the case of Turner, even his unkemptness, churlishness, his incorrect speech, and (following on the love-affair) his misanthropic hatred of any kind of social contacts, proved of advantage to his work and so to mankind generally. Self-consciously aware of his limitations, his disinclination to go out and about to routs and junketings, or upon the tipsy week-long sprees which were a feature of his age, not only kept his nose more closely to the grindstone, but preserved that sturdy health of his which enabled him to achieve so enormous an output.

Would that his boyhood friend, Girtin, had been rescued by any such brake upon his dissipations. Born with the silver spoon of genius in his mouth, his easy breadth of rollicking good-nature enabled him to retain the friendship of Lord Elgin and the Earl of Essex, while turning night into day with wild companions like Jack Harris, the frame-maker of Gerrard Street, who marketed his work, and kept a tavern-club, or the dissolute George Morland, the portrayer of homely rustic scenes, and most English of painters despite the French blood in his veins, whose career of prodigality is unique even in the annals of Art.

The artistic reputation of the cheerily improvident Girtin had, in spite of his reckless indifference to material ambitions, gone up by leaps and bounds since his path last crossed Turner's. When, in 1799, his faculty of working unperturbed in the noisiest surroundings led to his starting a sketching-class, his prestige and popularity drew many influential names into his circle. The coterie met at each other's houses in turn, and the host of the evening, in exchange for hospitality and materials, retained all the work done. Girtin was most eager to include Turner in the band, but Turner always steadfastly refused, partly, doubtless, out of disinclination for any society but his own, or

68

maybe from dismay at the expenditure called for on his evenings as host. Besides, any sketches he made could command ready cash, instead of becoming forfeit for unappreciated entertainment.

In 1800 Girtin's worldly circumstances considerably improved with his marriage to the only daughter of Mr. Borritt, a rich goldsmith in the City, who was devoted to his brilliant, happy-go-lucky son-in-law, and to all intents and purposes adopted him. Girtin had remained friends with Paul Sandby, the R.A., now seventy-five, who had taught Turner water-colour, and upon his marriage became a neighbour of Sandby's, removing from Drury Lane to St. George's Row, Tyburn, or St. John's Wood, as it was afterwards named, where, we are told, 'his house, like his heart, was open to all'. The name Tyburn came from a rivulet, the Tye, which had its source where Fitzjohn's Avenue meets Lyndhurst Road, and fed the marshy land which was converted into the lake in Regent's Park. Contrary to popular belief, it was here that Tyburn Gallows stood, and it was removed several times before coming to its final site at Marble Arch.

As Girtin never studied his own best interests by painting in oil before 1801, he never attained Academy rank, for in this year he showed signs of consumption and was ordered to Madeira. Before leaving, this extraordinary genius, who had painted scenery for Covent Garden, completed in distemper an enormous semi-circular panorama of London, over nineteen hundred square feet in area, which was exhibited in

Spring Gardens, Admission 1s., his studies for which are to be seen in the Print Room of the British Museum. In Paris, on his journey to Madeira, it became evident he had not long to live, so he remained there for six months, his brilliance unimpaired by his disease, and made some of his very finest drawings for his faithful benefactor, the Earl of Essex.

Meanwhile, Turner had been paying a first visit to Scotland. Apropos of one of his water-colours made there, *Norham Castle*, he in later years passed the same ruins, and swept off his hat to them. His companion, Cadell, the Edinburgh bookseller, asked him why.

"I made a drawing of it some while back," replied Turner. "It took; and from that day to this I have had as much to do as my hands could execute."

His original journey to Scotland was made by collier, and, by mixing with the crew on equal terms, he was able to add to his expert knowledge of the anatomy of ships and their conduct in all kinds of waters and weathers. The humble mode of life that he preferred brought him in touch throughout his life with practical people, whose technical information was of inestimable use to his art as a seascape painter. While he was away consorting with grimy stevedores and deckhands, the august Governing Body of the Royal Academy elected him a full Academician. The year was 1802; Turner was twenty-seven; and the honour reflects almost equal credit upon that discerning Council of Academicians as upon the artist.

The subject of his diploma-picture, traditional in manner, was *Dolbadern Castle, North Wales*. Since it is customary to associate the name of Turner with that of Ruskin, and to suggest that without the writer's aid the painter would never have achieved immortality, it seems a suitable occasion to remind the reader that it was not until Turner was in his sixty-eighth year that Ruskin, then a youth of twenty-four, published one word regarding him. Without diminishing Ruskin's assistance in popularising Turner's work among the general public (which I am by no means convinced is in any way important) it strikes me that a man such as Turner, who was A.R.A. at twenty-four and R.A. at twenty-seven, had little need of dilettante boosting half-a-century later, after his life-work was completed and he had bequeathed it to the nation with £140,000 of hard-earned money. I would even hazard the suggestion that the boot was on the other leg, and that Ruskin would long have been forgotten had he not ridden to notoriety on the shoulders of the greater man.

In the Academy catalogues from 1791 to 1801 the artist's name is merely given as W. Turner, A.: henceforward he became Joseph Mallord William Turner, R.A. I seem to perceive Turner's own hand in this, for we have the temperate Stothard's authority that his head got slightly swelled by the distinction. He curtly refused after his election to abide by the customary courteous practice of visiting his electors in gratitude for their suffrages.

71

"If they had not been satisfied with my pictures, they would not have elected me," he insisted. "Why then should I thank them?"

But that this same ungracious boor could be sensitive and considerate is shown by his taking his father to live with him in Harley Street in that same year, soon after his demented mother had been removed to her last home in Bedlam. Six years previously the Tory Government had imposed a tax on wig-powder, with the result that gentlemen began to wear their own hair, thus depriving barbers, William Turner among them, of their chief source of revenue. From then until his death in 1830 the old man lived with his celebrated but manifestly un-snobbish son on the happiest terms, saving the pennies by waiting on him, answering the door, stretching his new canvases and varnishing the completed paintings, so that Turner was wont affectionately to declare: "My father begins and finishes my pictures for me."

In the same year Turner made his initial trip to the Continent, only newly accessible to Britons after the period of war upheaval. One fancies he must have originally been impelled by the ready sale likely to accrue from picture-souvenirs of that Grand Tour which was then an essential part of a cultured person's education. Apart from innumerable sketches, later put to good use, he brought back his vigorous and finely-composed *Calais Pier—English Packet Arriving*, which Ruskin subsequently declared to be 'the first which bears the sign manual and sign mental of

Turner's colossal powers'. A contemporary critic similarly hails his advent in 1802—'A new artist has started up—one Turner. He had before exhibited stained drawings, but now paints landscapes in oil; beats Loutherbourg and every other artist all to nothing.' The new note struck was, above all, that of truth and the absence of theatricality in the portrayal of the elements, and in *Calais Pier*, it may justly be said, Turner first got home to the public at large, instead of being recognised for what he was by the art-world alone.

Turner continued on through France to Switzerland, from which visit his Alpine studies emanate. The foreign place-names in the titles of these subjects are frequently mis-spelled by him. From his *Val D'Aosta*, dated this same year, we may also deduce a momentary dive into Italy, though his serious incursions did not take place for sixteen years to come.

History does not record whether he passed through Paris, where Girtin, now dying, nevertheless continued, we learn, 'to draw till within a few days of his death, though he was so debilitated that he could scarcely hold his pencil'. One must assume that 'Honest Tom's' rich father-in-law, Phineas Borritt, was temporarily estranged from him, possibly through some scape-grace prank of the wild young painter. That he did not predecease his former favourite we know, from the fact that he could never afterwards refer to him without weeping. Whatever the reason, there is abundant proof that as his end approached,

73

money was short with Girtin, for when he came back to England to die in the autumn of 1802, it was to the house of his brother John, the engraver, in Castle Street, Leicester Square. This brother lives unpleasantly in our recollection as having rushed to the dead painter's home as soon as the breath was out of his body, and laid claim to all he could find there in consideration of cash-advances. This though Girtin's wife and child were left without resources.

Girtin died at twenty-seven, an irreparable loss to British Art. An anonymous donor erected a monument to his memory in St. Paul's, Covent Garden. The association of that church with Turner—it was there that his parents were married and buried, and he himself baptised—leaves little doubt that the unknown was he. The secrecy was like him: he had ever been the staunchest admirer of the dead man, who had been his first and greatest friend. He always afterwards spoke of 'Poor Tom' with a sigh, delighted in the golden light-effect of what he called 'Poor Tom's yellow drawings', and persisted that Girtin's masterpiece, *Chelsea Reach looking towards Battersea*, excelled anything he himself had done up to that time.

"I would have given one of my little fingers to make such a one," he declared.

Girtin's rare combination of dexterity and sincerity is as discernible in the early Cathedral Series as in his later and bolder work, with its rich tones and dashing line. The chief difference between his art and that of Turner is that Girtin, while lacking

74

Turner's gift for detail and general imaginative quality, had greater powers of virility and selection, as well as mastering very much more quickly those luminous colour-effects in which Turner, conceivably inspired by him, finally attained sublimity. It is symbolic of the difference in their natures. While Girtin seems to have been happy in his friendship with the greater master, we have no evidence of his appreciation of the other's work, while Turner from the first perceived and unenviously lauded Girtin's originality and brilliance.

Girtin's erstwhile teacher, Edward Dayes, who had caused him to be committed to Bridewell, could not in his jealousy allow the dead to rest, but published a violent assault on the recently-deceased Girtin and his work. This, coming at a time when all the art-world mourned its tragic loss, brought about a boycott of Dayes' business as a Perspective-Tutor, ruined him financially and socially, and caused him to commit suicide within two years of the death of Girtin. About the same time, by an extraordinary coincidence, the Castle Street premises of Girtin's engraver brother were destroyed by fire, depriving him of his irreplaceable stock-in-trade, and causing the death of his sick wife from exposure and shock.

CHAPTER IV

1803-7

WHEN Turner was elected R.A. his official portrait was painted by his brother-Acamedician, George Dance (afterwards Sir N. Dance-Holland, Bart.). As in all the other representations of him, the prominent nose and pertinacious chin leap primarily to one's eye, but in this case we get an impression fuller than usual of his hair, which is rendered as coarse and thick, and long enough to be tied with a ribbon at the back. The slovenliness of garb for which he afterwards became famed had evidently not manifested itself in 1802, for Dance depicts him with a flowing white cravat and positively dashing cape and coat-lapels.

The public recognition of his talent brought him many opportunities of widening his social circle, but he could hardly ever be induced to come out of his shell, and his habit of never answering invitations, but just putting in an appearance or not as the spirit moved him, must have rendered him the less welcome in the houses of new acquaintances. Apart from his disinclination for society in any form, his concentration upon his work, his application to both money-getting and the mastery of his craft, became more and more intense. He was not a quick learner: it was only by dogged perseverance that he turned his natural gifts into achievement: and the only way he knew was that of the labouring-men from whom he sprang—to get up early in the morning and toil hard all day. Similarly, the saving of money had by now become an instinct: he had originally started putting by for his marriage, and so got into the habit.

Among all historical examples of dual personality Turner's is surely the most striking, in that he presented to the world-at-large one odd and possibly unattractive character, while gradually revealing to his critics, brother-artists, and all those who had eyes to see, susceptibility to feel, and brains to understand, that he was also a supreme poet and inspired visionary. His spiritual and aesthetic intellect, unsurpassable in range and brilliance, retained its fire up to the very hour of his death, when his artistic aspirations still sought the attainment of the intangible. His other mundane brain simultaneously remained throughout his life little more than mere provincial common sense, slow in the uptake, suspicious, unhumorous, and stingy. How many North-countrymen has one heard say "All Ah know is that twelve pence mak' wan shillin', an' twenty shillin's mak' wan pound, and that's enough for me", in tones of self-congratulation, positively boasting of their limitations? Well, Turner was like that: with the earthy side of his thinking apparatus he was ever on the watch for people who might try to get the better of him. He not only prided himself that he could not be caught for a farthing, but even, in true plebeian fashion, thought himself clever if he could do down the other fellow, instead of being ashamed of it, or, better still, considering dishonesty beneath his dignity. But then, on his worldly side, Turner had no dignity, despite the fact that dignity, nobility, and grandeur are the keynotes of his work. His work, however, was the product of his intellect and sensibility, and the only part it had in the unwashed, mean, myopic human shell was that, through neglect of his person and indifference to mankind, he had more time and energy eft for the creation of immortal masterpieces.

It is essential to recognise and accept this unique duality at this early stage of Turner's existence, when with his feet about to be planted firmly and of his own choice in the gutter, his soul coincidentally commenced to follow its own brave mystical call. It was the period of life at which, with all normal humans, the problem of sex raises its provocative head, and Turner was more highly-vitalised and virile than the next man, even if it were not clear from history that creative genius craves emotional stimulus in full measure. Turner's filial and home relations show that he was naturally domesticated, and the ardour displayed in preparations for his intended wedding gives one justification for believing that normal married life with a wife of his own class would have satisfied his physical needs. With artists, oftener than other men, the spirit can only soar when the flesh is released from its craving. The attractive Girtin had, we learn, prior to a happy marriage denied to Turner, 'taken his fun where he found it'; but the uncouth barber's son, shy, tongue-tied, unhappy in Society, had no such opportunities. It is the less surprising, therefore, to discover that it was Turner's wont, right from the time of his thwarted love-affair, to work hard from Monday morning till Saturday night, and then button up a five-pound note in his breast pocket, disappear without explanation to his father into mysterious resorts in Deptford, Billingsgate, or Wapping, and return to his work after the week-end with zest renewed and the new clean eye of every painter's predilection.

From boyhood on it had always been the shipping areas that attracted him, and the society of fisher-folk that he preferred. On colliers and the boats of rum-smugglers he was in his natural element. A common man himself, and as English as he could be, he there mixed with the coevals of the earthy half of him, and the sailorman's happy-go-lucky sexual morals would naturally appeal to a simple rough chap unfitted for fleeting lyrical romances. The physical grossness and coarseness of the women in his pictures either reveal his instinctive preference, or indicate the class of female with which he habitually associated. But the lily that rose upon those dunghills of the docks was that through his intimacy with seafaring life he was to become unquestionably the greatest seascape-painter that has ever lived.

We shall find for a while this sensual urge somewhat

complicating his existence, but since it is the root-cause of inconsistencies in Turner's nature which have mystified posterity, it needs to be faced boldly at this point, in order that it may subsequently inter-fere no further with the story of his life than it did with that life itself. In the many monographs and biographies of the painter which I have studied in order to say what I have to say, I have found none which treats his life, as differentiated from his art, and particularly his sex-life, chronologically. Where the authors have not hypocritically evaded the ugly issue altogether, they have either veiled it in depre-catory innuendo, or so skipped about from one decade to another as to leave the impression that their central figure was abstemious, celibate, and chaste until his dotage set in. It is my purpose to persuade the reader that from early manhood until old age his secretiveness and love of seclusion was largely due to the fact that he had something to conceal, that he started early to lead a double life, and was obstinately determined it should appear a single one, whatever other eccen-tricities were ascribed to him

Almost immediately after moving from Hand Court to Harley Street, we find a second address printed in the Academy catalogue— 75 Norton Street, Portland Road. Of this new domicile, off Fitzroy Square, the only details to hand are that it possessed a gallery at the back whence intending purchasers were con-ducted by Turner Senior to see his son's pictures . . . for which services, if legend does not lie, the old man

TURNER AT 22

SELF-PORTRAIT

(Tate Gallery)

was not above pocketing shilling tips. It has puzzled many previous writers that though, from the time of his election as a full Academician, Turner was most conscientious in his attendance at the regular meetings, and, when in the company of his brother-artists, could be genial and even jovial, they were never invited back to his home, the very whereabouts of which was left mysterious, as the catalogue's two simultaneous addresses indicate. He similarly no longer associated with Dr. Monro, who did not die until thirty years later. That his disinclination to return hospitality was not due to his being ashamed of his humble parent is manifest from the fact that it was always the old fellow who welcomed buyers and agents at the house, and that he raised no objection to the ex-barber continuing to attend professionally certain favoured customers.

Not even meanness accounts for his pointed evasions, for I shall show later that, with his brother-Academicians at least, he could on occasion be hospitable. No: the true reason was that in his studio at Harley Street Turner had for the first time employed a housekeeper, a music-teacher's widow named Sarah Danby, who through propinquity had inevitably become his mistress. The elder Turner seems to have uncritically accepted this, and sundry similar backslidings, as just his son's queer way, part and parcel of one he single-mindedly loved. Sarah had a niece, Hannah Danby, who in 1801 was sixteen, and who within two years had displaced her aunt as the favourite of

Turner's seraglio. We shall see much of Hannah in the years to come, and the fact that she was subsequently an idle and forbidding slattern is as undeniable as that in after years her features were rendered uninviting by a cancerous disfigurement so marked that she was constrained to wear big bonnets to conceal it. But both these distinguishing characteristics may have come into being later, like her two illegitimate daughters. Owing to Turner's impenetrable reticence we cannot tell; any more than we can discover whether, as some allege, Turner's first few abodes boasted some degree of comfort, instead of the depressing squalor which later so unfavourably impressed all visitors.

One thing is certain. None of the painter's artist-associates were invited to Norton Street, and Hannah Danby was the skeleton in the cupboard. It must not be forgotten that Turner was proud and sensitive, and not at all the man to wish to expose publicly his weakness for illiterate females of the servant-class. Nor yet the man, if I read him aright, to subject his promoted domestic to the indignity of being quizzed and sneered at by his swagger friends. His partiality for that type of female remained with him till death, and though its increasing embarrassments brought him the solitude he courted, it must, by cutting him off from refined and intellectual circles of society, have been responsible for keeping him the ignoramus he remained.

There are many indications that he would, if not so handicapped, at any rate have associated a good deal more with his friends on the Council of the Academy, of which he was for fifty years an active member, being indeed for a long time one of the unpaid Auditors. He was simple-mindedly proud of the distinction, a loyal upholder of the Institution's prestige, a tactful peace-maker in heated disputes, and punctilious in the performance of his official duties, however distasteful, in which category must be included his Visitor's Lectures to the students. These, like his speeches at the regular meetings, were as much an agony to him to prepare and deliver as they were to listen to, being 'confused, tedious, obscure, and difficult to follow', apart from the indistinctness and frequent inaudibility of the speaker. His life-long friend, the sculptor Chantrey, subsequently founder of the Chantrey Bequest, was wont to say: "He has great thoughts, if only he could express them." The 'great thoughts' in question were, apparently, solely connected with Art, as his contributions to discussions on business and money-matters were not only unacceptable, but sheerly incomprehensible.

That in spite of his home environment he retained the aspiration for the accepted forms of culture is proved, not only by his marked preference for classical and mythological themes and settings, but by the poetic quotations he added, in and out of season, to the titles of his pictures. He was an early admirer of Sir Walter Scott, who in 1803, the time of which we write, had just issued his first original work, "Minstrelsy of the Scottish Border ", his previous two volumes having been merely translations from the German. Henceforward, also, the painter was for forty years to come to jot down from time to time fragments of an ambitious projected epic-poem of his own, "The Fallacies of Hope", which was never published, and never deserved to be, consisting as it did of an ungrammatical farrago of romantic flapdoodle, but excerpts from which were subsequently attached to many of his exhibited works. We learn also that in the painter's sparse impedimenta on his sketching-tours was always included the same small travelling-library, comprising a translation of Horace, Young's "Night Thoughts", and "The Compleat Angler" of Izaak Walton—the latter not unexpected in one who was himself an ardent fisherman from boyhood.

The mention of rod and line brings us further corroboration of the Danby ménage, in that, although Turner's own homes were taboo to his intimates, he was by no means averse to spending holidays in the country-houses of his friends, particularly when there was good fishing to be had; and that on such visits he was a cheery, sociable soul, utterly different from the grumpy recluse to whom the art-world was already growing accustomed. He even bowed enough to conventions to travel with a carpet-bag, instead of carrying his personal belongings in a handkerchief as heretofore! The opening of the nineteenth century saw the commencement of his life-long intimacy with Mr. Walter Ramsden Fawkes, the Squire of

Otley, near Harrogate, whom he had met on his Yorkshire sketching-tour, and whose house, Farnley Hall, grew year after year fuller of Turner's work, so that not less than £10,000's worth remained there after the painter's death.

The year before Buonaparte declared himself Emperor, our peace with France came to an end, the menace of invasion hung over England, and the Continent was closed to Turner until 1815. His Swiss study exhibited in 1804 must certainly therefore have been painted from sketches made previously, as became his habit. In the intervening period until Waterloo he concentrated on his own country for his subjects and backgrounds, and very frequently spent long periods with the hospitable Walter Fawkes at Farnley. He was extremely popular with Fawkes' young family, and was known to all and sundry as 'Little Turner'. When not playing with the children, or being the life and soul, so we learn, of picnic-parties, he fished in the Wharfe, shot grouse on the Yorkshire moors, and made innumerable sketches of the mansion and its grounds. We read of his umbrella being blown away, and of his trundling, chuckling, after it: we hear also of his driving a merry party home over rough ground, upsetting the chaise in a ditch, and being thenceforward nicknamed 'Over-Turner'.

That he could similarly shed his taciturnity and reserve when with trusted friends is shown by his attachment to the family circle of Wm. Frederick Wells, President of the old Water Colour Society, and

later associated with Turner over the latter's *Liber
Studiorum*. Wells' eldest daughter, who became Mrs.
Wheeler, and continued to know Turner until they
were both old people, was in childhood the little girl
who handed up materials to the boy Turner when he
climbed a tree to get a better view. In early manhood, Turner, she tells us, 'usually spent three or four
evenings in every week at our fireside: . . . I can still
vividly recall my dear father and Turner sketching
or drawing by the light of an Argand lamp, whilst my
mother was plying her needle, and I, then a young
girl, used to read aloud some useful and entertaining
work.' She goes on to say that 'of all the light-hearted,
merry creatures I ever knew, Turner was the most so',
and describes how she came in one day to find the
house in mirthful uproar, and Turner on his knees in
the drawing-room, romping with her little sisters, who
were pretending he was a horse, and driving him
with his voluminous cravat for reins.

In 1804 occurred the death of Immanuel Kant, the
philosopher, and also of 'Madcap' Morland, the whilom
friend of Turner and Girtin. This delightful painter,
after a life-time of wild dissipation and consequent
vicissitudes, became partly paralysed, and, being
incarcerated in a sponging-house upon the suit of a
publican-creditor, was in the act of attempting to make
a drawing whereby to discharge the debt, when he was
seized with an attack of the brain fever from which he
died, followed only three days later by the death from
heart-failure of his lovely, young and devoted wife.

After 1804 Turner never exhibited water-colour in the Academy, more's the pity. Nor elsewhere, for the rules of the R.A. vetoed the public display of any member's work in other galleries, except those of the British Institution. His work was still subject to the imputation of being under the influence of Wilson and of Claude; and his output in the year just mentioned was comparatively small, consisting as it did of *Narcissus and Echo*, and a number of engravings of Scotland, Berkshire, and elsewhere; but 1805, the year of Scott's "Lay of the Last Minstrel", the battles of Austerlitz and Trafalgar, and the death of Nelson, showed a remarkable advance, not only in activity, but quality.

Both 1800–10 and 1800–20 are variously named by the pundits as marking the artist's 'First Period', and in either case we have already seen it ushered in with his triumphant *Calais Pier*. The favourite *Garden of the Hesperides*, sombrely magnificent, further consolidated his rising reputation; but far more significant were the flood of masterly sea-pieces now due to be recorded. "Vandervelde—I can't paint like him," Turner is reputed to have declared, but in everybody else's mind he had by now left Vandervelde far behind. His rival water-colourists he had easily outclassed; it was the turn of the oil-painters to be vanquished.

For some while past his critics had complained of the topographical inaccuracy of his work. His pictures, said they, did indeed give wonderful *impressions* of the places represented, but were demonstrably wrong in detail. One is irresistibly reminded of the type of army-officer who, after witnessing some epoch-marking production of a Shakespearian play, can only comment afterwards that the baldricks were worn wrong, the poetic genius of the dramatist and the interpretative art of the actors being completely above his head. Henceforward Turner, now very much his own master, was to discard all attempts at petty verisimilitude, and concentrate upon the gods of his idolatry—distance, mystery, and light. The new note is struck in 1800–2 with his *Caernarvon, St. Donat's*, and first *Pembroke* studies, and thereafter is increasingly insistent in his work.

Now for the first time he commences to sketch in oil out of doors, and his old love, the Thames, seems by his output to have claimed much of his time, for in the next few years, come, hot-foot, the uniformly masterly *Sheerness, Pilot Hailing a Whitstable Hoy, The Nore*, and *Meeting of the Thames and Medway*. Turner's deliberate throwing overboard of all reality, as such, brought him further adverse criticism with one of his very greatest seascapes, *Shipwreck*, now in the National Galley, and even more drastic disapproval, particularly from naval men, in respect of his enormous canvas, to be seen in Greenwich Hospital, of the 'Victory' at Trafalgar. It was painted to the order of George III as a companion-picture to de Loutherbourg's representation of *The Glorious 1st of June*, and Nelson's Flag-Captain, who is inevitably best known as 'Kiss me' Hardy, declared it was 'more like a street-scene than a battle, and the ships more like houses

than men-o'-war'. It is said that while painting it
Turner was harried perpetually by clever-clever arm-
chair-critics in uniform, and one may candidly admit
that His Gracious Majesty had selected the wrong
artist if a photographically literal souvenir of the
battle was all that was required. With regard to that
indubitable masterpiece, his *Shipwreck*, referred to
above, this was bought by Sir John Leicester, but he,
influenced in all probability by ignorant popular
opinion, did not care for it, and exchanged it for *The
Sun Rising through Vapour*, which Turner re-purchased
in 1829 and presented to the nation at his death.

The last-named picture was always one of the
artist's own favourites, probably because it, though
imitative and unremarkable otherwise, introduces
almost for the first time in his work that imaginative
effect of radiance in the sky after which he so per-
sistently strove, and which was subsequently to hall-
mark the very greatest of his pictures.

Both Pitt and Fox had died in 1806, the year before
Pall Mall became the first street in the world to be lit
by gas, *The Sun Rising through Vapour* was exhibited,
and Byron's first published volume, "Hours of Idleness",
appeared. In the same year the Council of the
Academy appointed Turner Professor of Perspective,
a post he continued to hold, in name at any rate,
for thirty years. That he was gratified by the distinction is manifest from his adding the letters P.P.
to his R.A. in the Academy Catalogue. That he was
not a success in the position can be foreseen, for, as

Bernard Shaw has pointed out, 'Those who can, do. Those who can't, teach'. Turner was essentially a doer, and, being always at a loss for words at the best of times, manifestly not a preacher. That he possessed the necessary knowledge, we have proof: that he was conscientious, we can readily believe: but that he could clothe his theories in language comprehensible to the student is rendered even the more improbable when one recollects his previous failures as a drawing-master, and as a speech-maker at Academy Council-meetings. He seems to have done his best Perspective-tuition by blackboard demonstration, and to have diminished any risk of unintelligibility by committing his discourses to paper and reading them aloud to the class. On one occasion, however, the manuscript was mislaid in a hackney-coach, and so there was no lecture that day. Another time, he dismissed the students on the plea of 'domestic affliction', though Hannah Danby might not have recognised herself from the description! In spite of everything, however, Stothard, by now R.A., made a point of attending the lectures. Though too deaf to hear the discourse, there was so much to *see*, he said, so "much that I delight in seeing".

Far more significant that same year was the commencement of the artist's celebrated *Liber Studiorum*. The roots of this vast undertaking can be traced to two of Turner's ineradicable faults—his jealousy of any artist whose work could be construed as rivalling his own, and his petty-minded determination to prove publicly that he was the better man. Right up to the commencement of his Italian pictures his purpose was liable to be deflected by outside influences in a fashion well-nigh unbelievable, considering his position and distinction. His abiding envy of the popularity of Claude, the painter of Lorraine, is shown by his very Will, wherein he directed that two of his favourite pictures should only become the property of the nation if hung in the National Gallery between two of Claude's which he considered over-rated. But as early as 1806 the accepted mastery of the earlier artist had already begun to irk him, and the successful publication twenty years previously of a collection of Claude's drawings under the general title of *Liber Veritatis* had long caused him to toy with the idea of issuing a similar work which should excel in every way its predecessor, and incidentally demonstrate the inexhaustible versatility of J. M. W. T. The instinct of challenge likewise fitted in with a project he had in mind, of making more and quicker money by appealing to the public direct, and thus raking in the profits of publisher, printseller, and agent, as well as artist.

The inception of the project dates back to the autumn of 1806, in the cottage at Knockholt, Kent, occupied by Mr. W. F. Wells, in whose home-circle Turner was always welcome, as we have previously seen. I quote Mrs. Wheeler, Mr. Wells' daughter, once more. Her father, she says, 'had for a long time urged upon Turner the expediency of making a selection from his own works for publication, telling

him it would surely be done after his death, and
perhaps in a way that might not do him that justice
which he could insure for himself . . . Turner at
length gave way when he was staying with us in Kent
(he always spent a part of the autumn in our cottage).
He said: "Well, Gaffer, I see there will be no peace
till I comply; so give me a piece of paper. There
now, rule the size for me and tell me what I am to
do." My father said: "Well, divide your subject into
classes—say pastoral, marine, elegant pastoral, and
so forth": which was accordingly done . . .'

The 'and so forth', we may add, subsequently
included Historical, Mountainous, and Architectural,
in Turner's advance publicity, where the work was
described 'Intended as an Illustration of Landscape
Composition'. But whereas Claude's work had
merely consisted of swift brown-wash records of each
of his major works as completed, made solely for
identification, and never intended for publication,
Turner's Balzacianly grandiose scheme was to issue
with the utmost pomp and splendour one hundred
magnificent engravings of elaborate sepia-drawings by
himself, in serial parts of five plates each, of the same
same size as the drawings, displaying a breadth of
range in style and subject never hitherto attempted.
The magnitude of the enterprise, one not quite fair
to Calude's far less pretentious effort, was such as to
keep him busy for full twelve years after its actual
commencement in 1807. Turner at first decided to
do the etchings himself and entrust the engraver's

work to F. C. Lewis, one of the finest aquatinters of his day, at five guineas a plate. With the very first subject, *Bridge and Goats*, however, he changed his mind, instructed Lewis to etch as well as engrave, and when the aquatinter understandably charged him three guineas for the extra work, quarrelled with him and transferred the job to Charles Turner, who, though his namesake, was no relation. Charles Turner was not only one of the most distinguished of contemporary mezzo-tinters, but also the most prolific, for in his eighty-five years he is credited with an *œuvre* of nearly 700. He is said to have taught J. M. W. T. the engraver's process of scraping a plate. His bargain with the artist as regards the *Liber* was that he should be paid eight guineas per subject, the sum refused to Lewis. This arrangement continued with twenty of the fifty plates he had contracted for, when he too retired, after another sordid dispute with the pub-lisher-artist on money-matters, an estrangement con-tinuing for nearly twenty years. Two likenesses by him of his famous namesake are in the National Collections.

The disputes with engravers were by no means ended, at least five others being commissioned and discarded at Turner's caprice. There is no possible question but that J. M. W. T.'s commercial morals were those of the petty-tradesman who never misses any chance of cheating which presents itself. Before attaining a position of power he was always grumbling about being under-paid, but was the very first on becoming an employer to do unto others as he would not they should do unto him. He would vary an agreement to his own advantage while denying an equal right to his co-signatory. His shiftiness and abysmal meanness in money transactions appeared to him fair-trading, but he was not nearly so good a business-man as he flattered himself, and the highly-advantageous proposition of the *Liber* was a financial failure owing to Turner's muddleheadedness, lack of method, and inability to play fair by either his fellow-craftsmen or the public. With his subscribers to the serial-issue, who were required to pay £17 10s. for the privilege, he was flatly dishonest. Not only were the issues unpunctual, the whole series being suspended for three years on end, but the advertised cost was raised, and retouched impressions of the worn plates were frequently and deceitfully substituted for early, fine ones. The quality of the paper and binding was cheese-paringly poor, and not as guaranteed, and many serial parts were sold short of the number of plates announced. This last fraud, we learn with interest, was due to Turner trying to save money by having the covers stitched at home by his female domestic (none other than Hannah Danby) who abstracted proofs here and there to sell in the vicinity for the pin-money quite evidently denied her by her master. This was not the only instance of the *Liber's* biter being bit, for Turner's flat refusal to pay discount to book-agents and retail-tradesmen, and his short-sighted reluctance to advertise properly, circumscribed his market, and the blundering venture, after floundering on haphazardly, capriciously, till 1816, expired at the fourteenth number with only seventy-one of the hundred projected plates finished. The remaining twenty-nine were completed by 1819, though never published.

The painter's dual personality is perfectly epitomised in the *Liber*, which, commercially an egregious fiasco for which nobody else could be blamed, was, as Art, an outstanding triumph such as no other living soul could claim. Books have been written about it, whole chapters devoted to it in the biographies, with only occasional dissentient notes in the general chorus of enthusiasm. Although, to pursue the Balzacian simile, it proved eventually to be as formless as the uncompleted "Comédie Humaine", it would have been considered, in the case of any other artist, to be ample life-work, and was, at least at that time, quite comprehensively the 'Illustration of Landscape Composition' which it set out to be. It is also, as Turner intended, a summary of all those varied phases of his art which did not include colour, and was fully up-to-date in harnessing his new theories of atmosphere, distance, light, and mystery to his acknowledged mastery of topography, architecture, and nature generally, whether water, sky, and fire, or trees and rocks and hills and table-lands. Of the hundred plates the most notable, or at any rate the most generally esteemed, are *Dunstanburgh*, *Morpeth*, *Norham* and *Hornby* Castles, *Little Devil's Bridge*, the *Wye* and *Severn and Wye*, *Peat Bog*, *Rizpah*, *Alps from Grenoble*, *Solway Moss*, and the individual, though gloomy, *Jason*.

Every quarter-inch of any of them, or any other of his drawings, will, as Ruskin claims, bear the test of the magnifying-glass.

But with impressions so unequal in quality, isolated plates came into demand among collectors, much to the resentment of Turner, on his artist's as well as his tradesman's side. "What is the use of them," he angrily demanded, "except together?": and there is in W. P. Frith's Autobiography a delightful anecdote of Turner, seeing one such single *Liber* proof in the Oxford Street shop-window of Halstead, the print-seller. Bursting in, he commenced to rage and storm at the dealer for the stained and battered condition of the plate. Halstead, justifiably incensed, asked him who the devil he was, and, on being informed, responded tartly: "Well, Sir, I have long desired to see you, and now that I have seen you, I hope I shall never see you again, for a more disagreeable person I have seldom met."

Despite Turner's every effort to injure himself with well-wishers, the monetary value of a complete set of the *Liber* rose to as much as £3,000 within his lifetime, and 'single impressions are known to have fetched as much as two hundred guineas'. After his death the bulk surplus of unsold and unissued *Liber* stock realised £18,000. The proofs remaining to Charles Turner alone brought that engraver £1,500, while many similar impressions, discarded by him as lumber, had been used for lighting fires. The aged mezzo-tinter is reported to have exclaimed with tears in his eyes: 'Why, good God, I have been burning bank-notes, all my life!"

CHAPTER V

1808–13

WORK on the *Liber Studiorum* continued, as has already been remarked, until 1819, and the whole story of its inception, construction, publication, and associated meannesses, eccentricities, and vicissitudes has only been given in continuous narrative so that the reader may see it in proper relation to Turner's life and art-career.

We must now revert to our true period, 1808–9, when in the great world outside Turner's orbit, poor 'Farmer George' III lost his eyesight as well as his wits; Tom Paine exercised the Right of Man to die; Scott published his "Marmion" and Byron his provocative "English Bards and Scotch Reviewers"; and Drury Lane Theatre was destroyed by fire. News of the last being brought to its proprietor and manager, Sheridan, in the House of Commons, that body immediately adjourned in sympathy. Sheridan hastened to the theatre, but, perceiving it was doomed, sat quietly watching the conflagration from a coffee-house opposite, while discussing a bottle of port, with the comment: "It's hard if a man cannot drink a glass of wine by his own fireside."

There is some slight connection between Drury Lane and Turner, for de Louterbourg, with whom

G

97

he was so recently associated over their companion battle-pieces for Greenwich Hospital, had been a scene-painter at 'the Lane', and it was now, when Turner was thirty-three, that his admiration of the highly theatrical artist influenced him to rent a house near de Loutherbourg at West End, Upper Mall, Hammersmith. Mrs., Mme., or Frau, de Loutherbourg emerges from and retires again into historical obscurity with the episode of her showing her resentment of Turner's too-frequent visits by slamming the door in his face, declaring angrily that he had already picked up too much from her husband. This may account for his being only temporarily in Hammersmith. That the lady's accusation may have been founded on fact is indicated by his undisguised 'borrowing', in his work of the period, of figures and architecture from the Old Masters, including a scaffolding from Rembrandt.

The fact that from now on his previous domicile in North Street, Fitzroy Square, disappears from the Academy Catalogue, while 64 Harley Street remains in addition to the new Hammersmith abode, proves to me that he had in the meantime purchased the Harley Street premises (as we know he did some time or other) and had temporarily let them while waiting to buy adjoining properties, in order to build behind them a studio-gallery, where his pictures could be displayed to potential buyers. We have already seen that in North Street there was such an apartment, and the same applies to his latest house in Upper

Mall, where, in what he delighted to call his 'Turner Gallery', he exhibited his *Shipwreck*, *Death of Nelson*, *Sun Rising through Vapour*, and other marine-subjects, including his immortal *Boat's Crew Recovering an Anchor*. The reader is already aware, through the *Liber*, that Turner was abortively seeking to cut adrift from middlemen in the way of topographical-publishers and picture-agents, and by these display-galleries of his he hoped similarly to dispose of his oil-paintings and water-colours direct. In Upper Mall he was successful, finding purchasers for many of the above sea-pieces in Fawkes of Farnley, Sir John Leicester of Tabley, the noble Lords Yarborough, Lonsdale, and Harewood, and George, third Earl of Egremont.

The home in Hammersmith had the additional attraction to a disciple of Izaac Walton of having a garden which ran right down to the river, and we hear of the new tenant both fishing and sketching from his own boat, and leaving his water-colour studies to dry on the floor of the summer-house, 'as he could see them there'. We learn also that he kept a bay pony and gig, and was wont to drive, noticeably slowly, round the near-by countryside with his father (but never Hannah Danby) as companion, hob-nobbing with roadside acquaintances. The old hairdresser by now had developed a nervous tic or twitch, which startled strangers. The pony, Crop-Ear, was a bit of a character also, to match the odd household. Turner, who loved all animals, was devoted to it, and boasted that it never got tired and could climb hills like a cat; but the animal was obstinate and self-willed, rejected its master's affection, and did exactly what it pleased.

Turner, on returning from Spithead a year or two before, inspired by seeing the victorious British battleships which had captured the Danish fleet at Copenhagen, had told a friend in a rare burst of expansion and enthusiasm that he had decided to devote himself for a period to depicting 'Simple Nature'. In these years round 1808–9–10, in addition to his labours on the *Liber Studiorum*, we get the first-fruit of his resolve in the intimate and serenely masterly landscapes, *Windsor*, *Abingdon*, the two *Walton Bridges*, *Trout Stream*, *Landscape with Cattle in Water*, *Windmill and Lock*, *London from Greenwich*, *Sandbank with Gipsies*, and, above all, *Bligh Sand*. This phase of wholly un-affected delineation of typically English scenes in all weathers, each lovelier than the last, is, indeed, accepted by some as 'the essential Turner', and continued right on to *Frosty Morning*, in 1813.

Another companion of his jaunts in the pony-trap was the Secretary of the Academy, Henry Howard, and together they went out to Heston to see Howard's acquaintance, the Vicar there, the Rev. Henry Scott Trimmer, a man of about Turner's own age, and a lover of Art, who was to become a life-long friend. At that very first visit Turner seems to have consulted him about episodes in Ovid and other classics for projected pictures. The clergyman also had a family, and Turner, who always liked children, and got on with them, found the society of the youthful Trimmers so delightful that the drive to Heston was repeated. On the road from Hammersmith Turner espied a cottage on a plot of land between Twickenham and Isleworth which took his fancy. Though he did not use it for some years, he bought the property. Just as he had come to Hammersmith to be near de Louther-bourg, so the proximity of the Trimmers now attracted him. Right from his Brentford schooldays, also, these stretches of the Thames had particularly called to him.

When one recollects that at this very period Turner was showing the petty and untrustworthy side of his nature in the publication of the *Liber*, it is surprising to find him simultaneously taking pleasure in the society of old friends as well as new ones like the Trimmers.

In 1809 we find him staying at Petworth Park, the Grinling Gibbons-decorated seat of his patron, Lord Egremont, with its exclusively British Art-Gallery, glorifying the work of Gainsborough, Reynolds, Romney and Hoppner as well as Turner. Other guests were his Brother-Academicians, the plump and jovial sculptor, Chantrey, and George Jones, the soldier-artist, who so prided himself on his resemblance to the Duke of Wellington that the wags advised him, on the day of the Iron Duke's funeral, not to go out, lest he got buried in error. Turner himself is at this time described as 'the very moral of a master-carpenter, with lobster-red face, twinkling staring grey eyes, white tie, blue coat with brass buttons, crab-shell turned-up boots, large fluffy hat, and enormous umbrella'. The Earl, his host, seems also to have been a bit of a 'card', the father of four illegitimate children, whose mother he married so that a fifth might be born in wedlock. Just the man, indeed, to understand and appreciate another oddity like Turner. Each as self-opinionated and pig-headed as the other, they were always engaged in friendly disputes. One time it was as to whether carrots floated, so the vegetable and a bucket were sent for and proved Turner right: they did float. Another argument arose about how many front windows there were in a certain house in the neighbourhood, and a post-chaise was summoned to take them immediately, to settle the question.

The painter was provided with a painting-room to himself, and did the bulk of his work before anyone else was up; so that he had the reputation among his fellow-guests, who saw him fishing during the day-time, of being idle. His *Petworth*, painted there, has a significant sub-title 'Dewy Morning', and he probably in the same studio completed *Tabley*, *Cheshire*, also dated that year. As ever, nobody else was allowed to enter his Sanctum Sanctorum. If the Earl wished to converse with him, he had to give a pre-arranged knock as signal, when Turner would unlock the door. The cheery Chantrey somehow learned the password, and, imitating their host's gait and cough in the corridor, effectually obtained admission, which became a perennial jest between them. George Jones, the other

R.A. guest, was laid up with a bad leg while at Petworth, and speaks of Turner's eager kindness and sympathy; adding that when he went fishing with Turner (who had 'the worst tackle in the world') the latter, though always successful, would scrutinise each fish as caught, from the point of view of whether it was not so small that it should be put back in the water. We also learn that, while at Petworth, the clumsy fellow spilt tea over a lady-visitor's frock, and gave her a small drawing in compensation.

Two of his very greatest masterpieces now appeared, the vigorous and sublime *Spithead, Boat's Crew Recovering an Anchor*, with grand figure-studies, deemed by many to be his most complete and satisfying work, and the superb *Wreck of the 'Minotaur'*, painted to the order of Lord Yarborough, which W. L. Wyllie, R.A., himself a marine-artist, has declared to be 'the most splendid sea-picture that has ever been painted'. The artist was the first to render waves abounding with life, and to capture for his canvas the virility of the winds as they master the protesting sails.

The same date brought *Lowther Castle* for the Earl of Lonsdale, while round about then, Paul Sandby, Turner's old teacher, died at the age of eighty-two, Abraham Lincoln, Tennyson, Gladstone, Darwin, Elizabeth Barrett Browning, and Cardinal Manning were born, 'The First Gentleman in Europe' became Prince Regent, Napoleon married Marie Louise, Edmund Kean took his first London benefit, and the book-reviewers were busy with Scott's "Lady of the

Lake", Miss Mitford's "Our Village", and Jane Austen's "Sense and Sensibility".

It was in 1810 that Turner paid the first of three visits to the Isle of Man, bringing back with him some Manx cats for Hannah Danby. 1810 also saw one of his prolonged visits to the Fawkes family at Farnley Hall. Hawkesworth Fawkes, the eldest son of his host, was his especial favourite among the young people, and was perpetually at Turner's elbow while the artist sketched on the banks of the Wharfe, or noted down impressions of the flower-garden, the Cromwell relics, the oak-panelled rooms, old staircase, and made a hundred other souvenirs of the pleasant, friendly home. Major Fawkes, the Squire's brother, was writing a book on the plumage of birds, for which Turner made twenty coloured illustrations, including a grouse, peacock, heron, dove, and game-cock, on one occasion going out on to the moor and shooting a cuckoo to use as a model. The hospitable Walter Fawkes made a sketch of his famous guest which was 'thought by friends to be very like', representing him as 'a little Jewish-nosed man in an ill-cut brown tail coat, striped waistcoat, and enormous frilled shirt, the feet and hands notably small, sketching on a small piece of paper, held almost level with his waist'.

We learn that he found time so frequently to visit the village ale-house that he ran up a score of four-pounds-odd, and, disinclined to settle in cash, gave a valuable drawing which the publican later disposed of to Fawkes.

To Farnley we owe not only sketches. One of the artist's most masterly and virile sea-pieces, *A Ship of the Line* (or alternatively, *First Rate*) *Taking in Stores*, regarding which one never finds a disparaging word, was designed and completed in water-colour in a single session of three hours, after breakfast, at Otley Hall. Though full of intimate naval detail, and embodying a rough sea and sky, it was made entirely from memory, and shows no sign of haste. Walter Fawkes was present throughout the entire achievement, and speaks of the inspired frenzy of the artist at work. Immediately it was done, however, host and guest went out shooting together.

Hawkesworth Fawkes' boyish idolisation of the cheery, playful 'Over-Turner' unknown to London Art-Circles, continued through the years, and it is to him that we owe many manifestly authentic anecdotes of the painter. One such speaks of the inception of the tremendous *Hannibal crossing the Alps*, exhibited 1812.

'One stormy day at Farnley,' says the younger Fawkes, referring to 1810, 'Turner called to me loudly from the doorway, "Hawkey! Hawkey! Come here! Come here! Look at this thunderstorm. Isn't it grand? —isn't it wonderful?—isn't it sublime?" All this time he was making notes of its form and colour on the back of a letter. I proposed some better drawing-block, but he said it did very well. He was absorbed—he was entranced. There was the storm rolling and sweeping and shafting out its lightning over the Yorkshire hills. Presently the storm passed, and he finished.

'"There, Hawkey!" said he. "In two years you will see this again, and call it 'Hannibal Crossing the Alps'."'

Having conquered the sea, he now set himself to master the field of pure imagination. At the appointed time *Hannibal* duly appeared, a dramatic triumph, with the dispirited Carthaginians filing through a ravine, and the storm breaking above. The Hanging Committee of 1812 apparently did not appreciate the magnificently effective work at its true worth, for they 'skied' it over one of the doors, in spite of Turner's indignant protests. Some unwieldy verse was appended to the picture, the first public excerpt from the painter's own fatuous poem, "The Fallacies of Hope" already referred to:—

' Craft, treachery and fraud—Salassian force,
  Hung on the fainting rear! then Plunder seized
  The victor and the captive—Saguntum's spoil,
  Alike became their prey; still the chief advanced,
  Looked on the sun with hope; low, broad and wan.
  While the fierce archer of the downward year
  Stains Italy's blanch'd barrier with storms,
  In vain each pass, ensanguined deep with dead,
  Or rocky fragments, wide destruction roll'd.
  Still on Campania's fertile plains—he thought,
  But the loud breeze sobbed, Capua's joys beware.'

The sample is rather above the average of the 500-odd lines preserved of the uncompleted 'epic', of which eighty or so were at different times inserted in the Academy Catalogues. In addition, the artist frequently took for subjects of his pictures episodes in the unpublished poem, and announced them as such, without any further explanation, lyrical or otherwise. Did he intend to print the ambitious work one day, illustrated by reproductions of the paintings? Since it never came to pass, visitors to the Academy must have been considerably mystified; but perhaps less mystified than if they had had to wade their way through those reams of doggerel, as I have. Even apart from its bathos and incoherence, faulty spelling, grammar and punctuation, its many gaps through illegibility, the wretched thing is so abysmally dull. That Turner was proud of it, and unaware of any shortcomings, is clear from his continuing to add to it, year after year, and quoting from it, relevantly and irrelevantly, as a pendant to his pictures. Occasionally, as we come to such pendants, I will transcribe them, to demonstrate their ineptitude. That will be sufficient to indicate yet another queer quirk of the painter's, without administering the whole long sleeping-draught to the reader.

In the previous year, Turner exhibited quite a number of works based on classical legend, including the peerless and arresting *Apollo and the Python*, with its striking colour scheme and perfect draughtsman-ship. Here, as also in *The Garden of the Hesperides*, the vivid imagination of the painter is exemplified by his conception and convincing interpretation of the

mythical monsters introduced. It was at this particular Annual Display that he happened on a young
artist named Bird, disconsolate because no room could
be found on the crowded walls for his first accepted
work. Turner removed one of his own from a good
position and presented the vacant space to the aspirant.
Only a great man could have done so: and this,
remember, was the same jealous sharp-practitioner of
the *Liber Studiorum*, still in publication, the same person
who (render it consistent if you can) at this very time
refused to turn out his tenants in Harley Street when
their rent was a year in arrears, but gave them further
time to pay.

Sir Walter Armstrong speaks of this period as the
happiest of Turner's life, and one is constrained to
agree when one reads of his first visit to his 'native
heath', Devonshire, in 1812, the year marking the
birth of Dickens, Napoleon's retreat from Moscow,
and the publication of "Pride and Prejudice".

The tour was probably originally planned through
tentative commissions for "Cooke's Southern Coast",
not commenced till 1814, and the present-day reader is
lucky in having Mr. Cyrus Redding, whom Turner
met in Devon, to give an intimate pen-portrait, made
on the spot, of the artist at work and play. On this
trip the painter accepted only casually the proffered
hospitality of the nobility and gentry, preferring to
follow his own devices in the old sketching-tour fashion
—getting up early, covering much ground on foot,
keeping himself to himself, and swiftly filling a myriad

to him that its walls were covered with paintings by
Angelica Kauffman—nymphs, and men like nymphs,
as effeminate as possible. I directed his attention to
them, and he wished me "Good night in your
Seraglio!"'

Except on this tour, Turner seems never to have
mentioned his Devon origin. He told Redding he
was a Barnstaple man, and Redding accepts it as
gospel, but, according to me, Turner's gift for picturesque exaggeration was merely being stimulated
by the fact that South Molton, the abode of his grand-
parents, is in the Barnstaple district. Probably
prompted by the same association, Turner's only
known move towards making contact with any of his
relations took place on this tour. Some years before,
an uncle of his, Price Turner, of Exeter, had sent
some sample drawings made by his son, Thomas Price
Turner, to J. M. W. T., in the hope of advancing the
youngster's prospects, but evidently without arousing
the painter's interest, for he left the matter to Old
Barber William to deal with, and the youth subsequently studied music instead. Now, however, being
in the neighbourhood of Exeter, Turner had the whim
to call, and did so, characteristically excusing himself
on the grounds that his old father had wished it. After
a short interview with Price Turner, his daughter,
and son Thomas, all connection between the painter
and his relatives ceased for more than twenty years,
an undeniable fact afterwards distorted by the
Exeter Turners from motives of cupidity.

Turner's financial circumstances in 1812 were such that he felt justified in purchasing the house in Queen Anne Street, Portland Place, where by a coincidence his friend, W. F. Wells, had been at school, numbered at that time 47, and now 23. By doing so he was able at last to satisfy his ambition of erecting a 'Turner Gallery' adequate to the private display of his work, for the new abode communicated at the back with his two properties in Harley Street, though he did not own the corner house in between. With the acquisition of the third domicile, he commenced to rebuild quite elaborately from his own plans, and was extremely niggardly and truculently distrustful respecting the bills for reconstruction.

John Martin, a contemporary artist, speaks of 47 Queen Anne Street as 'gloomy, detached, five-windowed and large-doored'. The same large doorway, designed by Turner, still stands to-day. The painter was to reside there, on and off, for thirty years to come, and, even when living elsewhere, used the picture gallery, with Old Father William as custodian. We know that Hannah Danby, graced with a courtesy Mrs., was permanently in residence, for visitors henceforward speak of being scrutinised suspiciously from the area by an unprepossessing female in a large bonnet, and of the hallway and gallery being infested by mangy Manx cats, described by the artist as the pets of his housekeeper. There is no information forthcoming as to whether the lady had, during the intervening decade, been a victim of the fell disease

which left her face disfigured, though one might
assume so from her perpetually wearing that large
bonnet, as we know she did.

Nor, since Turner wrapped his grim home in such
mystery that it might have been a coiner's den or
Witch's Sabbath Chapel where Black Mass was
celebrated, can we tell whether the still youthful
housekeeper had by now fallen into the sluttish habits
which later made this very house a byword for squalor
and depression. Perhaps it was a first outcome of
her illness that she became slack and careless, a second
outcome that the loss of her beauty rendered her no
longer attractive to Turner, with the third outcome
that she retaliated by becoming indifferent to him
or his comfort. It seems the human explanation:
Turner was emphatically not the man to turn her
adrift, and she not improbably the woman to take
full advantage of the fact, embittered and resentful
as she may understandably have become. It cannot,
at the same time, have made Turner's life any the
easier, nor caused him to re-consider the question of
introducing her to his friends. I cannot conceive that
the idea of marrying her had ever entered his mind.
Even without that, he had, as I see it, a Mrs. Caudle
at home, perpetually carping and reproachful, who,
as far as one can gather, merely cooked the dinner,
for we know it to be Old Father William who did the
shopping and answered the door. When one con-
siders the spectacle of our poet and visionary tied in
Unholy Wedlock to an illiterate, no longer comely

shrew, his happy holidays with friends become as natural as his growing relapses to the bottle, and the re-commencement of his periodical disappearances at week-ends into Wapping, with the famous buttoned-up five-pound note.

What we do know about the Queen Anne Street house at this early stage was that the entrance hall, adorned by a Reynolds, and various casts from the antique, gave a vista of stark rooms unfurnished save for stacked and uncompleted canvases, and admitted on the right to a sombre little dining-room. His work room, formerly the drawing-room of the house, was on the first floor, had no skylight, and led out of the newly-erected Picture Gallery. The entrance was obscured by a large screen, behind which Turner was wont to listen, unperceived, to criticisms of his work. On one occasion two visitors, anxious to discover for themselves whether or no it was the truth that for some of the more delicate effects in his oil-paintings, Turner used water-colour, were about to make a test with a damp finger, when Turner burst forth from concealment like an angry bear.

The merest glimpses only were obtainable of the interior of the workroom, so jealously were its secrets guarded by the owner, but we know that on a circular table always lay his gloves and neck-kerchief, besides his colour-box and palette, the latter a mere square of wood with a thumb-hole. His brushes were equally primitive, and many of them practically hairless. He possessed no mahl-stick, never feeling the need of one, so steady was his hand. He used principally cobalt, gamboge, smalt, verditer and different ultramarines, and liked to have his dry colours rubbed freshly on the palette each morning with cold-drawn linseed oil. If the result was not to his liking he would demand angrily of the studio-boy, his father, "Can't you set a palette better than this?"

As some slight concession to conventional ideas of hospitality, there stood, on a rickety dresser in the Picture Gallery, a decanter of sherry and a single glass. Near it lay his travelling library, the Horace, Izaak Walton, and "Night Thoughts", while, in and amongst papers carelessly thrown down, were his flute and music. Amongst these loose manuscripts a visitor once observed a £200 Bill of Exchange, falling due that same day, the very existence of which had been forgotten by the painter, whose Art had temporarily got the better of his greed.

In 1813, when Livingstone was born, Napoleon abdicated, and "Home, Sweet Home" was first heard in the opera "Clari" at Drury Lane, Turner's phase of 'Simple Nature' came to an end with *Frosty Morning, Sunrise*. Sunrise—the artist's favourite working-hour. This pleasant pastoral, in the Dutch manner, now in the National Gallery, principally excited attention at the time for its convincing frost effect, now no longer visible. The model used for both the horses in the picture was the recalcitrant Crop-Ear, who continued to remain a protesting member of the family circle even after the Hammersmith house was vacated upon the death of de Loutherbourg. Turner told his friend Trimmer, the Vicar of Heston, that the original sketch for *Frosty Morning* was made by him in Yorkshire from a stage-coach shewn at a distance in the picture. In the youthful female figure depicted carrying the hare on her shoulder, Trimmer professed to see a resemblance to a young girl he had caught a glimpse of during a visit to Queen Anne Street, and he subsequently recognised the same form and features in the bucolic lass of *Crossing the Brook*. From the likeness to Turner, said he, he imagined her to be a relation. If the worthy parson is correct in his surmise, it is the only recorded personal contact with one of the painter's illegitimate daughters.

CHAPTER VI

1814–19

THE ex-barber now began to show signs of breaking up, and Turner, various instances of whose kindness have come under scrutiny, bethought himself of the land he had purchased at Twickenham as a fitting background for the old man's declining years. The accommodation in the cottage already standing there being insufficient, he caused it to be entirely rebuilt from his own designs, and once more, as in the case of Queen Anne Street, we are forced to Hardwick's conclusion that Turner would never have made an architect, for the new Twickenham edifice is described as an uninteresting plaster-covered villa of semi-Italian type, with iron steps and balustrade, erected on somewhat marshy ground. The property had previously been called Solus Lodge, but Turner found this too apropos, and re-named it Sandycombe Lodge. Here the painter stayed for a good part of each year till 1826. His father resided there continuously, but went up each morning to open the Gallery at Queen Anne Street on the chance of customers calling, a task which both parent and son evidently considered could not be safely entrusted to Hannah Danby, although she remained in town.

Through the absence of Hannah from Twickenham, the cooking and general domestic duties there devolved on Old William, but not only do I imagine that he liked it, but I feel certain that his son had foreseen he would, if only because it gave the old fellow occupation, made him feel he was wanted, and that his nose was no longer put out of joint by Hannah. On Tuesdays, that being Brentford Market-Day, he was often to be seen cheerily trudging homewards, carrying the weekly stores in a big blue neckerchief. The one thing that troubled him was that it was too far for him to walk to Queen Anne Street and back each day to open the Gallery, and he grudged his fare. Soon afterwards, however, he explained with great delight that he had found a way out, travelling by the market-gardeners' carts, sitting on top of the vegetables, in return for a tot of gin a day.

The old fellow began to make a garden out of the unpromising marsh-land, thick with willows, and spent much time digging there. Turner took an unexpected interest in the planning, and when his father constructed a water-lily pond, he himself stocked it with trout and carp from the neighbouring Brent. The ex-barber, it appears, also had ambitions as to extending the property, and quaintly commenced by annexing small portions of the public frontage, and fencing them in. The same, until brusquely reclaimed by the rural district authorities, were known to the local boys as 'Turner's Cribs'. These same irreverent urchins nick-named Turner himself

'Blackbirdy', because he stopped them rifling the nests.

The artist sat, rain or shine, on a kitchen-chair in the garden with a board for his feet, busy with the brushes while his father weeded and hoed near by. An experimenter all his life, he would at this period take up a position in a punt in mid-stream and paint from nature on canvasses as large as shrouds, tacked on broomsticks: rarely, however, completing such subjects, but rolling them up for further survey, which, they never got (*Gipsy Camp* being an exception), and starting on a fresh one. The boat from Hammersmith he now kept at Richmond, and when he wanted to go any distance, boatmen were hired to row him while he sketched. One such waterside-character at Sunbury, on being told that Turner was a great genius, refused to believe it. How could it be so, he demanded, when the man took out a bottle of gin with him, and got through it in a day, without offering the oarsman a single drop?

The friendship with the Trimmer family at Heston strengthened. The good vicar had not only a real understanding of Art, but was himself an amateur painter of talent. A sea-piece hanging in the vicarage about which Turner commented "I like that picture —there is a good deal in it," was painted by Trimmer himself, and there was at one time some talk of Turner giving the parson lessons, in exchange for instruction in Latin and Greek. As may be imagined, however, the artist did not prove an apt pupil, and was, moreover, always too occupied with some new subject for his brush. It is the vicar's own church which figures as an interior in the *Liber*, and when Mrs. Trimmer laughingly purloined one of Turner's sketches, he manfully masked his resentment, and made her a present of it, having first carefully made a duplicate for himself.

The Trimmer children, who made great friends with Turner, describe him as dirty and ugly, though kind and jolly, using the epithets 'pig-faced' and 'old', neither of which strike true, their visitor being sharp-featured and not yet forty. The vicar himself refers to him as neat but not smart, with gaiters to match his black clothes. He speaks of Turner examining an oil-sketch of Gainsborough's so closely by candlelight as temporarily to injure his sight.

Henry Howard, the artist who had introduced his fellow-R.A. to the family, was painting a full-length portrait of Trimmer's second son, then three, in a white frock and red shoes. Turner, looking on, seems to have been so unduly critical that Howard tersely invited him to do better. "This is what I would do," said Turner, and, wrapping the tabby house-cat's body in his own red handkerchief, he placed the animal under the child's arm, enormously improving the composition, not only in adding interest, but by repeating and fulfilling the colour-note struck in the shoes.

The young Trimmers recollect visiting the Turners with their father at Sandycombe Lodge, where the smallish rooms were decorated by models of ships in glass cases, the sea-backgrounds of which, Turner told them, he had himself supplied. When they stayed to a meal, though their hosts made them welcome, it was very much pot-luck, with currant-wine, two-pronged forks, clumsy rustic knives, and primitive crockery, on a rough table only partly covered by a cloth. At departure the children always had their pockets stuffed with cake by Turner. From their description it would appear, as one always surmised, that the great designer had no notion of applying artistic decoration to the home.

They speak of Turner fly-fishing for hours without result, but, when successful, giving them the catch; they recall, also, Crop-Ear, the horse (soon afterwards to strangle itself in its own chains at night, through an insubordinate disinclination to remain in its stable) and the gig in which they used to be taken for picnics. At Penn, in a field gay with wild flowers, Turner climbed into a ditch to sketch—to be out of the sun's rays, so he said: but to conceal his working-methods, hazarded Henry Howard, R.A., who was present. Turner and Howard were for ever disputing, principally over Turner declaring that the opinion of the public was not worth a rush, and Howard, as Secretary of the R.A., maintaining the contrary.

Turner wrote so few letters, beyond elaborately detailed instruction to frame-makers and engravers, that there has not previously been occasion to mention any, but now comes one which must be reproduced

verbatim, deficiencies in grammar, composition, punctuation, the use of capitals, and particularly in clarity,
included. Edited versions or part-quotations appear in
all the Lives, and in nearly every instance with the
avowed object of proving thereby that at forty Turner
had fallen in love again, this time with Trimmer's
sister-in-law.

'Tuesday, Aug. 1. 1815
'Queen Anne St.

'MY DEAR SIR,

   'I lament that all hope of the pleasure of seeing you
or getting to Heston—must for the present wholly
vanish. My father told me on Saturday last when I
was as usual compelled to return to town the same
day, that you and Mrs. Trimmer would leave Heston
for Suffolk as tomorrow Wednesday. in the first place,
I am glad to hear that her health is so far established
as to be equal to the journey, and believe me your
utmost hope, for her benefitting by the sea sir being
fully realized will give me great pleasure to hear, and
the earlier the better.

   'After next Tuesday—if you have a moments time
to spare, a line will reach me at Farnley Hall, near
Otley Yorkshire, and for some time, as Mr. Fawkes
talks of keeping me in the north by a trip to the Lakes
&c. until November therefore I suspect I am not to
see Sandycombe. Sandycombe sounds just now in my
ears as an act of folly, when I reflect how little I have
been able to be there this year, and less chance (perhaps) for the next in looking forward to a Continental

excursion, & poor Daddy seems as much plagued with weeds as I am with disappointments, that if Miss —— would but wave bashfulness, or—in other words—make an offer instead of expecting one—the same might change occupiers—but not to teaze you further, allow with most sincere respects to Mrs. Trimmer and family, to consider myself

'Your most truly (or sincerely) obliged,
'J. M. W. TURNER.'

Thornbury, author of the standard biography, interprets this, if you please, as 'the letter of an affectionate but shy and eccentric man, imploring his friend to help him at his need; talking of soon coming down again, but expressing his fear that he should never find courage to pop the question unless the lady helped him out'. He continues in maudlin fashion to speak of cruel Fate stepping in, leaving Turner 'to sink into the cheerless, selfish old bachelor, with no children to prattle round his knees . . .(!) with no hands save those of mercenary love to close his eyes and smooth his dying pillow'. It is not so much the writer's literary style one quarrels with, though it turns the stomach, as his main inference. For the life of me I cannot read more into the letter than that Turner was sick of Sandycombe, and hoped to get a tenant for it in the person of Mrs. Trimmer's sister, who had possibly dropped a hint that if it was in the market she might be a bidder. In Cosmo Monkhouse's largely impeccable Pocket Monograph, he seems first inclined to agree, and then throws the practical explanation overboard owing to an assurance by one of the Trimmer children, when grown up, that it was indeed a violent attachment. How was that infant to know, he who at the time of the letter described a Punch-visaged man of forty as 'old' and 'pig-faced'? Sir Walter Armstrong, on the contrary, has a solution so humorous that I wish I had the nerve to father it. If, says he in effect, there is more in the missive than an attempt to get rid of Sandycombe, it is a proxy-suggestion that the lady should dilly-dally no longer, but make up her mind to marry, not Turner himself, but his *father*, in which case the villa would be thrown in as make-weight!

I cannot believe that Turner ever wanted to marry anybody after he was grown up, and certainly not Mrs. Trimmer's sister. When I read of a later incident at an evening gathering in London, where, his roving and acquisitive eye lighting on some spectacularly well-made young woman, he nudged his neighbour and said "If she'd marry me, I'd give her a hundred thousand", I can well imagine his speaking the words, and even his playing momentarily with the idea of having an exclusive lien on the charmer, but even then I visualize the word 'marry' as purely, or impurely, figurative.

In 1814 Turner had only exhibited the two classical subjects *Apuleia in Search of Apuleius*, at the British Institution, and *Dido and Aeneas* at the R.A., the latter a dull work, possessed by what Ruskin calls the artist's 'brown demon', and not to be confused with the painter's other *Dido* picture, the important *Building Carthage*. 1815, on the contrary, was to prove a prolific and significant year. Of the eight pictures then displayed at the R.A., *The Battle of Fort Rock* is only remarkable for its sub-title quotation from the "Fallacies of Hope" MS.

'The snow-capt mountain, and huge towers of ice,
Thrust forth their dreary barriers in vain;
On the van progressive forced its way,
Propelled; as the wild Reuss, by native glaciers fed,
Rolls on impetuous, with ev'ry check gains force
By the constraint upraised; til, to its gathering powers
All yielding, down the pass wide Devastation pours
Her own destructive course. Thus rapine stalk'd
Triumphant, and plundering hordes, exulting, strew'd,
Fair Italy, thy plains with woe.'

To compensate, however, the same Catalogue announces the ever-memorable *Crossing the Brook*. This fascinating landscape, with its beautifully executed pine-trees in the foreground, is, in its technical mastery of the effect of great distance, not only the forerunner of Turner's romantic experiments in remoteness, but, in respect of colour also, marks the cross-roads where his earlier manner first branched off to that of his maturity. The influence of Claude is still apparent, and the name of the elder artist inevitably recurs in speaking of *Dido Building Carthage*, also shown this year, inasmuch as it and its companion-picture, *The Decline of the Carthaginian Empire*, exhibited 1817, both came into being through the same impulse of envious emulation of Claude which had prompted the *Liber*. The *Dido*, bold in its conception and fine mysterious expanse, is quite one of the best things Turner ever did in this style, though the small grouped figures and lofty Renaissance columns do give some slight justification for C. R. Leslie, R.A.'s allegation that it resembled the drop-scene of a theatre. It has never pleased the archaeologists, either: the old arguments of inaccuracy and unreality are trotted out, without taking into account that Turner was probably not only painting the scene as he himself preferred it, but also in the fashion in which he, as a tradesman, considered his customers would prefer it. As regards the latter he guessed wrong (though only temporarily, as we shall see) for the picture, painted to order for £100, was, after being abused by the Press, refused by the intending purchaser, and returned unsold from the Academy.

In the companion subject, *The Decline*, the same towering architecture and small figures occur, but the picture is of small importance, being, as Ruskin said, 'little more than an accumulation of Academy student outlines, coloured brown'. Curiously enough, Turner preferred it to its fellow at the time; but that he changed his mind is apparent, not only from the clause in his Will, where he bequeaths the *Dido* to the Nation on condition that it hangs next to a specified Claude,

but also by his attitude to Chantrey, who, courage-
ously uninfluenced by adverse criticism, made repeated
efforts to acquire it. Turner must have already decided
what he meant to do, but reticent, evaded the issue
by continually raising the price.

When it got beyond all reason, Chantrey demanded:
"Why, what in the world are you going to do with the
picture?"

"Be buried in it," grinned Turner. "I have
appointed you one of my executors. Will you promise
to see me rolled up in it?"

"Yes," returned Chantrey. "And I promise you
also that, as soon as you are buried, I will see you
taken up and unrolled!"

These two Carthage pictures, we are assured, were
conceived by the painter as political parables, intended
to warn England of her approaching ruin, sent to
punish her for revelling in luxury while France, the
bogey, greedily drew nearer. But then Turner was
always flattering himself that even his simplest and
most direct work held some marvellous hidden meaning.
Long after he had depicted Wyclif birthplace in a
sun-burst with geese in the foreground, he persuaded
himself that the geese represented ancient superstitions,
being driven away by the sun of the Reformation.
The Exile and the Rock Limpet is another example. That
was the unlettered hind trying his hand at rhetoric,
the author of "The Fallacies of Hope" at work, the
same barber's son, who from time to time, like Rembrandt before him, lapsed strangely into a preference

for the meretricious and the garish. After all, if one's taste errs in women, why not occasionally elsewhere? Even Homer nods. But just as Homer, or the syndicate of bards writing under that pseudonym, stands head and shoulders above all other poets, so we must be satisfied that in Turner, with all his blind spots, England can boast one of the very greatest painters that ever lived, the peer of Rembrandt, Michael Angelo, Titian, Raphael, and Rubens, and, in landscape-art, not only the greatest, but head and shoulders above all others.

It is the more needful to bear this in mind when one reads of his association with Cooke, the publisher, over the *Southern Coast* series, commenced just now. As Art, his forty contributions to the work—notably views of Lyme Regis, Falmouth, Clovelly, Minehead, Whitstable, and the Isle of Wight, in a comprehensive survey extending from Ramsgate to Land's End— were as worthy of him as his professional conduct in connection therewith was unworthy. Judging other people by himself, he accused Cooke of the very practices of which he himself was guilty as publisher of the *Liber*, and claimed as his right the same freedom of action which, also in the *Liber*, he had so strenuously denied to Charles Turner and F. C. Lewis. Though Cooke, who reveals himself in the correspondence as an entirely honourable and reasonable person driven to distraction by Turner, had guaranteed him £400 for the series at £7 10s. per drawing, Turner not only subsequently raised his price, first to £10, and afterwards to twelve-and-a-half guineas apiece, but demanded the additional fee for all the back drawings he had completed, delivered, and been paid for. Worse, he swore, if he didn't get the money, to start a rival *Southern Coast*. Plain blackmail, in short. He professed discontent with the letterpress, and proposed to write it himself, and only did not have his way because of the incoherence of his ungrammatical attempts. He demanded twenty-five sets of India proofs as a gratuity, but, after presenting a drawing to Mrs. Cooke as an olive-branch, changed his mind and demanded it back, with a fee of two guineas for the hire! While abusively insistent about getting his money on the nail, he put Cooke in hole after hole, by his unpunctuality and indifference; and when the long-suffering publisher, himself accused of bad faith to his clients through Turner's indifference, called in person to insist upon delivery of work long overdue, Turner wept crocodile's tears and said self-pityingly to Munro of Novar, who was present: "No holiday ever for me." That Cooke was stung into the use of the word "Rogue!", as we hear he was, can readily be believed.

The extent of Turner's shortsightedness in cutting off his nose to spite his face by thus maltreating publisers, engravers, and dealers is manifest when one realises that not only in the past had the vast bulk of his living been acquired through drawings and watercolours specially made for reproduction, rather than by the sale of his oil-paintings, but that for more than twenty years to come he relied, and had to rely, on the same source for his income. He was even constrained to accept further commissions from the hated but forgiving Cooke. After *Southern Coast* there is a continuous sequence of such serial issues with *Rivers of Devon* (1815–23), *History of Richmondshire* (1819–21), *Rivers of England* (1824), *Provincial Antiquities* (1826), and *England and Wales* (1829–38), Rogers' *Italy* (1833–5), Scott's *Works* (1834), and *The Rivers of France* (1833–5). And to the very end, as we shall see, our spoilt child remained greedy, suspicious, grudging, treacherous, underhand, mean, unpunctual, abusive, untrustworthy, obdurate, while continuing to consider himself hardly-done-by. But for his genius nobody would have bothered to put up with him, and, knowing this, he did not hesitate to take full advantage of the fact. Yet the actual handicraft continued consistently superb, the dual personality kept his Art immaculate while besmirching his good name—in very sooth a double life.

With the exception of the topographical work mentioned, nothing of the first importance from his brush was to appear between *Bligh Sand*, 1815, and *Bay of Baiae*, 1823; some consider, indeed, until *Cologne*, in 1825. The 'blight' that is so often said to have settled on his work during this decade can hardly be denied, in the face of *Waterloo* (1818), *Richmond Hill* (1819) *Rome from the Vatican* (1820) and *What you Will!* (1822). In this period, as well, we get the first positive proofs of a blight descending also upon his domestic and social existence, evinced by his indifference to the absence of any kind of cleanliness or comfort at Queen Anne Street, now that his father was no longer there. Their mode of life at Sandycombe Lodge was, as we have seen, that of peasants, but it was at least healthy and happy. At Queen Anne Street, on the contrary, neglect and squalor had by now taken a firm hold, so we learn from quite a number of unbiased witnesses, including the youthful Trimmers, though whenever they burst in upon the painter's privacy in London they were never allowed to leave without having their pockets filled with goodies. We hear of *Bligh Sand*, so much a favourite of the artist's that he refused to sell it, being used nevertheless to stop a broken window. The exterior of the house, dirty, silent, and forsaken 'like a bankrupt's warehouse', was never redecorated, as its neighbours were, and the only sign of life ever visible was a mangy tail-less cat lying asleep on a piece of ragged green baize in the area window. The railings and bell-chain were rusty; the door, apart from its grime, patchy for lack of paint; and the windows obscured by the dirt of years.

A chance visitor to the Gallery, after being left for a space in a dark, undusted ante-chamber, speaks of the Exhibition Room itself as cheerless, fireless, and uncared-for, with the cracked and broken skylight patched here and there with paper, quite ineffectively as regards keeping out the damp. There was a broken-down sofa, a common grained table, ramshackle buffet, threadbare discoloured drugget and shabby patchwork screen, all filthy. Leaning with their faces to the wall were stacks of canvases and murky-looking frames. All was litter, mouldiness, and confusion. Soot was everywhere, as were a small army of Manx cats, the only occupants of the apartments, save an unprepossessing female in an unwashed mob-cap.

Can one wonder that intimates were not invited there? May not even Turner, the champion despiser of appearances, have been as ashamed of his house as of his mistress? Hannah, it is true, cannot be blamed for the dilapidated outside of the house, but it was all of a piece with the dejected interior, for the state of which her sloth and slatternliness were indisputably responsible. The miser in Turner probably boggled at re-decorating the shell, knowing the kernel was irredeemably rotten. Or alternatively, the generally accepted view may be correct—that he simply did not care, and flatly preferred squalor to comfort, just as he preferred the Wapping pot-houses and brothels to Farnley Hall and Petworth Park. But did he? As I see it, he was naturally closed in, but always ready to be taken out of himself by jollity, camaraderie, or friendship, which could only happen when the money question did not intervene. We find him cheery and jovial and pleasure-loving with his father, with Chantrey and his brother-Academicians, with the Fawkes and Trimmer families, with Lord Egremont and every kind of common waterside character, male and female. I agree that Hannah may have had a lot to put up with, but I read nowhere of her good humour, and I have a notion that fun and laughter were the quickest way to Turner's heart. I question whether Hannah even 'fed the brute'. Perhaps she was a secret drinker, which would account for a lot. Hundreds of empty bottles were found in the house after Turner's death, and they can't have been his, because he was so rarely there. It gives one furiously to think. . . .

Meanwhile the great world was wagging briskly. 1815 had of course brought Waterloo, with Louis XVIII's return to the throne of France, and Napoleon's banishment to St. Helena. The next four years saw the publication of Keats' "Endymion", Shelley's "The Cenci", Mrs. Shelley's "Frankenstein", and Scott's "Rob Roy", with Byron's "Mazeppa", "Prisoner of Chillon" and the opening Cantos of "Don Juan". Also Jane Austen's "Emma" in the year before she died. Other memorable deaths were those of Warren Hastings, James Watt and Sheridan, by this time stout and mottle-faced. The celebrities born included Bismarck, Livingstone, Leech and Tenniel, Herbert Spencer, all three Brontë sisters, Thoreau, Walt Whitman, and George Eliot. One notes also the Cato Street Conspiracy to murder the Cabinet, and the retirement of John Philip Kemble, leaving Edmund Kean the acknowledged head of 'the' Profession. Kean just now founded a Bohemian meeting-place known as the Wolf Club, in the Coal-Hole Tavern, Strand, where relics are still to be seen. Tiny, even insignificant, with an unimpressive voice, he nevertheless gave such a terrifying performance at his first London triumph in 1814 as to throw Byron into a fit. His predecessor, Kemble, was of a very different type, cold, schoolmasterly, aloof, and not a favourite with his fellowplayers. The daughter of Lord North having conceived a passion for him, the nobleman offered the actor £5,000 to marry somebody else, anybody else. Kemble obliged, his wife being the widow of an actor named Brereton, but the Peer conveniently forgot his part of the bargain. More fortunate in the matrimonial stakes was Harriet Mellon, the actress, who about the same time married Coutts, the banker, only two months a widower, who within a very few years died and left her an income of over £70,000, thus enabling her in middle-age to wed the youthful Duke of St. Albans. Annals of the time would be incomplete without mentioning 'Beau' Brummel, who, though of humble origin, managed, even more through impudence than his nice taste in clothes, to become an intimate of the Prince Regent, who dressed coquettishly in public, though slovenly and dirty in his private life. 'Prinny', as ever, grew tired of his favourite, and dropped him. The court sycophantly following suit, Brummell returned, via a Debtor's Prison, to obscurity.

Three other sketching-tours now call for record, the first in Yorkshire, for the Rev. Dr. Whittaker's "History of Richmondshire". Of course Turner spent much time with the Fawkes family at Farnley Hall, where he was so taken by a patriotic song he heard that he copied out all its quite unremarkable verses in his sketch-note-diary. At another house where he was a guest there was an amusing contretemps owing to the host having been warned in advance by the correspondent who introduced them that the painter needed careful watching in money-matters. The actual phrase used was "Above all things remember that Turner is a Great Jew". Coupled with Turner's physiognomy, the epithet was taken literally, and when the family went to church on the Sunday, they pointedly left the artist at home. By an unfortunate coincidence, a fine hot ham was the principal dish at the midday meal, and in the hostess's confused apologies for such a lack of tact the mistake was eventually discovered.

The twenty water-colours he made for the *Richmond-shire* series, not issued till 1820, were not only of consistent excellence, but far more topographically accurate than usual, owing, it is thought, to the subjects having been selected for him by Dr. Whittaker, who travelled with him. Ruskin is enthusiastic about these drawings. 'The foliage is rich and marvellous in composition,' he writes, 'the rock and hill drawing insuperable, the skies exquisite in complex form.' Particularly notable are the various views of Hornby, the two *Richmonds, Easby, The Falls of the Tess, Aysgarth, Ingleborough* and, above all, perhaps, *The Crook of Lune.* It is alleged that eventually the greater part of £10,000 accrued to Turner for his share in the publication;

but it is perhaps a suitable occasion to note that, solely through his incessant labours, and the opportunities provided by his masterly treatments, the greatest school of British engraving came into being, from which emerged some of the most celebrated names in that branch of Art.

He had the great Sir Walter Scott as companion on his tour in Scotland for *Provincial Antiquities*, to which the novelist wrote the text. Scott, then making £10,000 a year, had no knowledge or appreciation of any art but his own, and seems to have been quite oblivious of Turner's distinguished position, let alone his genius, only accepting his services on sufferance 'because he was all the fashion'. If he had had his way he would ignorantly have chosen the Rev. Mr. Thomson of Duddingstone, who entertained the ill-assorted pair in Edinburgh, with Lockhart, Scott's biographer and son-in-law. Thomson himself was so conscious of his inferiority that it was with anxiety and trepedation that he exhibited his work to the R.A., but Turner, doubtless for Scott to overhear, merely remarked: "Hm . . . you beat me in frames. . . ." It is pleasant to remember that Sir Walter, towards the end of his life, was only too happy and honoured to know that Turner had consented to illustrate with a series of vignettes an authoritative edition of his collected writings. As well he might be, for, all else apart, in the exquisite medium of the vignette J. M. W. T. was the supreme master of all time. On the present tour, in 1818, just after "The

Heart of Midlothian" appeared, the novelist and the artist visited the scenes of a number of Scott's poems, Jedburgh, Dunbar, Linlithgow, Carlisle, and Stirling, as well as Edinburgh, resulting in imperishable souvenirs from Turner's brush, including *Edinburgh from Calton Hill*. At Smailhome the novelist told the painter that on these downs he had, as a lame boy, lain among the sheep and lambs, giving his mind 'a peculiar tenderness for those animals, which it had ever since retained'.

On leaving Edinburgh Turner had impressed upon the clerical illustrator, Thomson of Duddingstone, that, if the reverend gentleman were ever in London, he would be heartily welcome to a return of his hospitality at Queen Anne Street. On his next visit south, the clergyman took the painter at his word, and a date was fixed. It happened on the day appointed however, that Thomson visited a certain nobleman, who, upon inviting him to dine and being informed of the previous engagement, told him to bring Turner along also, instead of taking the meal at Queen Anne Street. When Thomson called and told J. M. W. T. of the new suggestion, the painter hesitated before accepting, muttering: "Well, if I must, I s'pose I must, but . . ." Before he could finish, however, Old Father William put his head round the famous patch-work screen, with an eager: "Go, Billy! Go! The mutton needn't be cooked!"

Turner's third expedition took him to the Continent, now accessible to Englishmen once more, and the best-known results are *Dordrecht* and *Entrance to the Meuse*, the latter being highly praised by some critics, and dismissed as unworthy of notice by others, equally emphatic. He also made an extensive tour of the Rhine, with a young Irish artist named Robert James Graves as companion. The latter describes how Turner would sit like an angler for days at a time facing a selected spot, with no more than the barest outline on his prepared panel, not working at all until some desired colour-concatenation occurred in nature, when he would cry "There it is!" eagerly seize his palette and brushes, and work frenziedly till the effect was secured. "I never lose an accident," was his mumbled explanation; but such divine accidents only happened to Turner. Graves avers also that, at their inn on the tributary Moselle, upon his enquiry at breakfast-time whether the absent Turner had as usual gone out early sketching, he was informed that Monsieur Turner had packed up and left for good at five o'clock, saying his friend would settle both bills.

I somehow don't think Turner liked Graves, who strikes one as a patronising sort of amateur, the type that is boastful about its private income. Not the man, one feels sure, to appreciate anyone who, like Turner, finished the day 'dizzy with work', after painting 'like a tiger'. There is a canvas of this tour, painted on both sides, because he could not spare the time to get another. It had to be displayed on an easel instead of being hung.

Turner returned home via Hull, and proceeded immediately to Farnley Hall, where, at the moment of being welcomed by Fawkes, he produced from his great-coat pocket a roll of more than fifty Rhenish drawings, selling the complete set then and there for £500. These exquisite works, executed with amazing rapidity, *Twilight in the Lorelei* being perhaps the *chef d'œuvre*, doubtless figured in the Water-Colour Exhibition which Fawkes gave that year at his house, 45 (now 35) Grosvenor Place. In the previous year, we learn from the diary of the second Mrs. Fawkes, the family were at Eton for the 4th of June—'to see the boat-race. Little Turner went with us.' It was about this time that Fawkes' eldest son, Hawkesworth, came of age.

In 1819, when the *Liber* was finally abandoned, Turner for the first time visited Italy, and it is notable that whereas he used water-colour for virtually all his studies of France, for those of Italy he almost exclusively worked in oil. Sir Thomas Lawrence is said to have been the instigator of the tour, and, if so, he introduced the Master to his spiritual home. Venice was not included on this occasion, so the artist's final and greatest stimulus was yet to come. But his National Gallery drawings of Naples and Capri, Florence, Rome and Tivoli, Lake Maggiore and Turin, form in themselves a complete summary of the artist's very finest qualities. Above all he brought back with him a new feeling for colour. Henceforward, marking the commencement in 1820 of his Second Style, his oil-

paintings no longer show the influence of Claude or
Wilson, the dominant dark backgrounds disappear,
the tranquil blues and greys and brows appropriate
to English landscape give place to the brilliant,
iridescent, and sometimes even violent, colouring
which was the peculiar secret and outstanding glory
of Turner, and has, indeed, become popularly synony-
mous with his name. This first tour in Italy planted
the seed of which we shall later see the leaf and
flower and fruit. There is a human sidelight on the
painter in the Academy Catalogue for the year after
his return, and only that year, where he proudly
adds to his R.A. and Professor of Perspective the
grandiloquent title, Member of the Roman Academy
of St. Luke.

CHAPTER VII

1820-30

IN 1820 poor George III died. In addition to all
his other ills, he had suffered continual biliousness
brought about through worry, and from the too-
strenuous exercise he took to guard against growing
fat. The same year saw the Bill of Pains and Penalties
to dissolve the new king's marriage to Queen Caroline
on the grounds of her sexual irregularities. When she
first arrived to defend her rights the populace were
sympathetic, but she soon made herself such a nuisance
that doggerel advice was chanted about the streets:—

> 'Gracious Queen, we thee implore
> Go away and sin no more:
> Or if that effort be too great,
> Go away at any rate.'

Fortunately for everybody, herself included, she died
in the following year, which also saw the death of
Napoleon at St. Helena. When they told George
that his greatest enemy was dead, he replied: "Is
she?"

George IV's coronation ceremony in 1821 was
unduly prolonged owing to the frequent retirement of
the monarch to King Edward's Chapel, the altar

of which was used as a wine-bar. His robe alone cost the country £24,000, the general expenses of the festivities being £243,388, as against £60,000 in the case of Queen Victoria. George's only child, Princess Charlotte, having died in 1817, her uncle, the Duke of York, now became Heir Apparent.

Scott's "Ivanhoe" and "Kenilworth" were published as were Shelley's "Adonais" and De Quincey's "Confessions of an English Opium Eater". Other contemporaries included Mrs. Siddons, the sister of John Philip Kemble, who is described at the time as 'almost Quaker-like in her simplicity', and as having, though advanced in years, a face which 'was wonderfully striking, in spite of a very evident moustache'. We read also, as a set-off to Turner's eccentricity, of Lady Hester Stanhope, then camping at the foot of Mount Lebanon, in hourly expectation of the Almighty's summons to her, as Queen of Jerusalem, to join the Congress of the Chosen. Eighteen years later she died in a tent, with thirty cats and the same number of servants around her.

Each time I have introduced morsels of English History into this book, in order to depict Turner 'in the round, warts and all', in proper relation to his epoch, it has occurred to me how extraordinarily English he was. In spite of possessing artistic genius, he had all our reputed national characteristics in an enlarged degree. He was slow in the uptake, suspicious of strangers, proud as Lucifer, he was certainly a member of the nation of shopkeepers, he muddled through, he even groused but paid. His very inconsistencies were British. The contrast between his constitutional niggardliness, for instance, and occasional bursts of generosity. . . . Someone who believed in him as a boy, and had bought his first drawings from the barber's door, fell on hard times, and was forced to advertise for sale the timber on his estate. Turner heard of it, and lent him sums amounting to £20,000, *anonymously*, and without security. It was repaid: but how many people would consider such a loan? To another who needed help he said: "Don't wish for money; you will not be the happier; and you know you can have any money of me you want." Yet this was the same Turner who, on receiving from a nobleman a generous cheque for a picture, scrutinised the figure discontentedly. "I've made it guineas, I think?" queried the donor. "Yes, but you've forgotten the six shillings for my coach-fare, coming here." Another time he was seen angrily disputing with an omnibus-conductor near St. Paul's. He had contracted to be taken to the Bank, and so would not pay a groat. We learn, however, that wherever he visited he left silver under his pillow for the servant; and hear of his roughly dismissing a beggar-woman, then running after her and slipping a five-pound note into her hand.

He was fond of quoting poetry, and delighted in playing the flute, we are told; yet was never happier than among the ruins and dirt of Wapping. He loved all animals and children, because he could not distrust them. He would play with them by the hour, but could be as brusque with the youngsters as with grown-ups when put out. To amuse one of them, he once arranged some red and green and yellow crystallised fruits in an elaborate pattern, wherein he become quite immersed. The child playfully scattered them, and was repaid by a scowl. "There, now! You have lost me fifty pounds!" grumbled Turner. He had been evolving a new colour-scheme.

Brusqueness: there are endless examples. What of the poor fat-headed lady with a pug-dog on her lap, who said he must really make her a pretty little picture of it? Turner, they say, went absolutely rigid as he icily replied: "Madam, you know not what you ask." Or the other simple-minded matron who protested that she could never perceive in Nature the tints Turner introduced into his landscapes? "How should you?" barked the painter.

We have seen how unexpectedly emotional he could be about the death of intimates, but when his colleague Haydon committed suicide, so far from showing regret, he grunted out repeatedly, "He stabbed his mother! He stabbed his mother!" because Haydon had attacked the administration of the Academy. Yet when somebody disparaged another artist's work, Turner would not allow it. "It is pretty," he said, "and he is a poor man with a large family."

He was a fantastic shambling slippered pantaloon with a misshapen umbrella that could be converted to a fishing-rod: but he was boy enough till the end of his life to push an old friend in a cupboard, lock the door behind him, and roar with laughter at the prank.

He would go over and over one of his large skies as many as nine times in order to get the required effect, and yet be Britishly impervious enough to smile when ignorant critics applied to the finished product their favourite, idle epithet of 'the slap-dash school', or enquired whether the picture had not by accident been hung upside down.

Those were the sort of catch-phrases slung at his *Bay of Baiae, with Apollo and the Sybil*, exhibited in 1823, the year after Shelley died at thirty, and " The Essays of Elia" were published. The *Baiae* saw the ushering in of the painter's new manner, an emotional impressionism expressed through vivid colour. The scene is pure phantasy, the mythology and archæology being demonstrably inaccurate. But the masterpiece of only a few years before, *Crossing the Brook*, is now left far behind; its tender tints and loving detail appear mild compared with the first example of the new phase of bold and courageous splendour. Seeming to summarise the painter's impressions of romantic and luxuriant Italy, and painted with masterly ease, this picture alone was sufficient to immortalise the artist, though even greater triumphs were to come.

George Jones, R.A., apparently recognised only the unreality of its treatment, for he chalked 'Splendide Mendax' on the frame. Turner merely laughed, and tolerantly let it stay there. Well he might, knowing what he had brought into being. It is from the Joneses and not the poets that one expects mere literal transcripts. It mattered no more than that the picture —recalling, as was truly said at the time, a window opened in the wall—returned unsold to the Queen Anne Street Gallery.

As in so much of the Master's work, including *Crossing the Brook* and *Frosty Morning*, the colouring described by contemporaries seems to have faded. In other cases it is so palpably the fact that their very intention has become obscure. Various reasons have been assigned—Turner's indifference, the addition of water-colour to oil bases, neglect of the paintings when completed, the absence of even rudimentary chemical knowledge in the preparation of the palette. At one time of his life, it appears, he did make some attempt to study the theory and science of colour, as variously propounded by Brewster, Goethe and du Fresnoy, but the general effect was that, while paying lip-service to two of those authors in titles to his pictures, he followed his own nose as usual. I was always, when an art-student, given to understand that Turner had been too hard up to afford proper pigments, but, now that I know better, I cannot help wondering whether the parsimonious creature did not content himself with inferior material from a short-sighted motive of false economy.

That he could withdraw with one hand what he could throw away with the other is proved at this period in connection with the foundation of the first British National Gallery in 1824. The present Trafalgar Square and Millbank collections were then initiated by the purchase through a Government grant of thirty-eight paintings, of which nine were British. A distinguished Committee, including Sir Robert Peel and Lord Hardinge, decided to approach Turner for the inclusion of his two companion *Carthage* pictures, the *Dido* and the *Decline*. The former, it will be remembered, had been so abused in the Press that the intended purchaser had refused to pay the agreed price of £100, and subsequently Turner had repeatedly rejected offers for it made by Chantrey. It, and the undeniably inferior *Decline*, were now considered by the National Trustees to be worth no less than £5,000, and a memorial was drawn up offering Turner that amount.

But the artist would have none of it. He was pleased and grateful for the gesture: for days afterwards he chuckled, "This is a great triumph!" but, having already decided on the *Dido's* future, he declined the £5,000 with apologies and thanks. "Tell the Committee," he directed their emissary, "that *Carthage* may some day become the property of the nation."

By accepting, the same result would have been obtained, with £5,000 in the miser's pocket: but no, the miser just did not choose to part with two of 'his children', as he was wont affectionately to call them. It was neither the first nor the last time he was to do likewise. All the same, a £5,000 offer for work rejected at £100 was indeed, as he so delightedly reiterated, "a great triumph!" Hawkesworth Fawkes, visiting London just then, speaks of his taking too much wine at dinner, and stumbling about afterwards, crying: "Hawkey, I am the real lion—the great lion of the day, Hawkey!"

Another lion of the day was Liszt, then paying his first visit to England. The original Drury Lane play-bill quaintly announces that he has 'consented to display his inimitable powers on the New Grand Piano Forte, invented by Sébastien Érard'. In the following year was published Chopin's Op. I Rondo in C Minor, and the Surrey Iron Railway was opened, the very first to operate, and running between Wandsworth and Croydon.

To Turner's work for the engraver must now be included seven illustrations of Byron. These subjects dealt with places he had never visited, like Athens, Malta, Rhodes, etc. Later he was able to work from photographs, but in 1825 the camera was only in the experimental stage, and Turner had unsatisfactorily to rely for his detail upon sketches by other people, who may easily already have claimed poetic licence to be inaccurate, before the Splendid Liar, Turner, got to work. Ignorance proved no obstacle to Turner, of course. As with his subsequent illustrations of Finden's Bible, what he did not know, he imagined. And if his improvisations occasionally represented Palestine or Greece as resembling Yorkshire, it was no worse than his transformation, in his *England and Wales*, of rolling downland into gloomy mountains, and parish churches into towering fanes. They were still genuine Turners, and the more so from their Apocalyptic unreality. The intention of the publishers of *England and Wales* was to present a comprehensive survey of our 'green and pleasant land', but a foreigner would get a very strange and false idea from perusing Turner's version, from which a large number of prominent cities, and even celebrated beauty-spots, are entirely omitted.

It was the same with his two *Rivers* series of England and France, in which no reference is made to the Thames, Mersey, Severn, Rhone, or Garonne, while minor streams and tributaries are elaborately treated, and the Seine is illustrated by a view of the Boulevard des Italiens! Turner had a plebeian taste for the bombastic, as we know, and there is little doubt that, under these high-sounding general titles, he issued collections of drawings which were merely elaborated versions of topographical drawings he had made, and sold, on his youthful sketching-tours. Finely imaginative, the majority of them, it is true, but simultaneously tradesman's work, a means of getting immediate and continuous cash without moving from the studio. It seems to me very significant that in those days Turner delighted to work whenever possible with the aid of a camera-obscura. I visualise his moving round that drum, and resolving to get *all* the view in, and probability be damned! And, on the top of that, a lot more still, out of his own head! That was the visionary: but the tradesman at this time once more kept bad faith with his public in his

Ports (subsequently *Harbours*) of *England*, the pre-
liminary announcement being worded with such
deliberate ambiguity that he could charge what he
liked, and end the series or continue it just as he pleased,
while many of the plates themselves were nothing
short of 'faked' by the introduction of high seas and
shipping to disguise the invisibility of the harbour
purporting to be represented. Authentic Turners, of
course, and better seas and shipping than anyone
else could do, but not playing the game, nevertheless.

Fawkes of Farnley, now about to die, came to
London to consult his doctor, and in the last few
weeks of his life Turner dined with him no less than
twelve times at Grosvenor Place. The passing of old
friends always deeply affected Turner, and in the
case of Fawkes, he could never subsequently be pre-
vailed upon to visit Farnley again, in spite of, or because
of, all the happy times he had spent there. Hawkesworth Fawkes, the son, however, remained one of
the few welcome visitors at Queen Anne Street (but
was never allowed to penetrate to the painting room),
and every Christmas, for twenty-four years, Turner
received from him a Yorkshire goose-pie, the replica
of one much appreciated by him when at Farnley.
All the correspondence and diaries of the deceased
were destroyed, so, as usual, we are deprived of
interesting data concerning Turner.

Various writers profess to find that the death of
Fawkes affected Turner so deeply that it was detri-
mental to all his subsequent work. I am quite unable

to follow this contention, with the very greatest triumphs still to come. That Turner's manner altered about this time cannot be denied, but I will not agree that the movement was retrograde, and must maintain that what change there was dated back to his Italian tour in 1819, and that his powers and energy were now in full flood. Thenceforward, as I see it, he determined to discard all precedent, and made it his business to astonish and dazzle the public with colour and attack, so that he might give them what he wanted, and allow his poetic imagination the utmost play.

The first fruit was *Bay of Baiae*, followed in 1826 by *Cologne*. Representing the arrival of a packet boat in glowing sunset, the latter dream-picture was declared by some ignoramus of the time to be uniformly coloured like the yolk of an egg. Its ideality and brilliance were so outstanding, however, to the discerning eye, that the P.R.A., Sir Thomas Lawrence, made a long face when he realised that it would competitively hang between two of his own portraits, of Lady Wallscourt and Lady Robert Manners, on the walls of the Exhibition. Turner perceived this, and with one of his rare impulses of generosity, darkened down the *Cologne* with lamp-black on Varnishing Day. When remonstrated with for having in mere caprice thus ruined a chef-d'œuvre, he merely chuckled.

"Poor Lawrence was so unhappy," he explained. "But it'll all wash off after the Exhibition!"

It was concerning this picture that the rumour

afterwards arose, causing consternation in Art Circles, as to it having been destroyed in a railway-accident, but it was happily a false alarm.

At the Academy foregatherings we frequently find the curmudgeon and miser decently human, and able to enjoy a joke, preferably of the schoolboy variety. When Stanfield's marine-piece *Throwing the Painter* arrived too late for exhibition, Callcott for fun produced a *Dutch Fishing-Boat Missing the Painter*, which Turner delightedly capped in the following year with his *Now for the Painter*, a seascape unremarkable apart from the jest.

Also with their humorous side are two other pictures of his that year, *Port Ruysdael* and *Mortlake Terrace*. As regards the first, 'there ain't no such place', the name as well as the scene being sheer invention; and, in connection with the latter, it being suggested to Turner that some dark object in the foreground would help his middle-distance, he cut out a dog in black paper and stuck it on.

At the convivial nights of the R.A. Club, held in the Thatched House tavern, he is described as thoroughly happy, 'a jolly toper', making feeble efforts to be funny, and laughing heartily at his own jokes. In his will he left £50 a year to the merry company, to be spent on an annual Turner Commemoration dinner, to be held on his birthday.

We find him painting at Cowes in the open, producing a finely sun-lit series of yachting studies, obviously a theme well-suited to him. In this year also, at the De Tabley Sale he repurchased for £514 10s. his *Sun Rising through Vapour* in order that it might hang, with *Dido Building Carthage*, between two works of the hated Claude in the National Gallery. History does not record whether he attended the auction in person, for he was wont to send the most extraordinary proxies to public sales, either to buy his work in, or to stop them being sold too cheap. On one occasion a cheery blue-aproned butcher-boy increased the bidding by five pounds a time before being asked for his credentials, when he produced a thumb-marked scrawl of authority from Turner.

Although Mrs. Trimmer's sister did not become the tenant of Sandycombe Lodge, Turner had by now disposed of it to a Mr. Ford. The change seems chiefly to have been dictated by the fact that Old Turner was on his last legs, and was perpetually catching chills in that marshy district. For his few remaining years he lived with his son and Hannah at Queen Anne Street, but he seems to have fought hard against the move, and ever after bitterly deplored the loss of his country 'estates'. Twickenham does not appear to have suited Turner's health either, for he is described as having grown 'as thin as a hurdle', a condition borne out by one of his rare letters, with its usual literary blemishes:—'Poor Daddy never felt the cold so much. I begin to think of being truly alone in the world, but I believe the bitterness is past, but has very much shaken, and I am not better for wear.' A deleterious effect of leaving Twickenham, however,

153

was that he was deprived of the humanisingly beneficial influence of the Trimmer family, and so became increasingly the slave of his own society and that of Hannah Danby.

Death had made havoc among the artists with Beethoven and William Blake; but Tennyson's first poems had been published, and Keble's "Christian Year". England could now even boast some sort of literary man as Premier, in the person of the capable and witty Canning, whose political verses were being widely quoted, such as:—

' In matters of commerce the fault of the Dutch
   Is offering too little and asking too much.'

Or his Needy Knife-Grinder with its famous conclusion:—

' I give thee sixpence? I would see thee damned
   first—
Wretch! whom no sense of wrongs can rouse to
   vengeance—
Sordid, unfeeling, reprobate, degraded, Spiritless
   outcast!'

The Duke of York now dying, the next in line of royal succession was his brother the Duke of Clarence, afterwards William IV. 'Our sailor Prince' some called him, because he had served under Nelson in 1788. With others less kind, his amiable chuckle-

headed inefficiency had earned him the soubriquet
of 'Silly Billy'. Under political pressure he had
married Princess Adelaide of Saxe-Meiningen, after
living for twenty years with Mrs. Jordan, the actress,
by whom he had ten children, thus founding the
noble family of FitzClarence. Rumour said that he
was unable to support his household on his £1,000
salary as Ranger of Bushy Park, and that he lived
on the actress's yearly earnings, which exceeded
£7,000.

In 1828 we find Turner in Rome again, following
the sun, that sun whose warmth and brilliance he was
to strive for the rest of his days to capture for his
canvases. Writing to the egregious Jones, and asking
to be remembered to 'that fat fellow, Chantrey', he
speaks of having been two months on the way:—'My
own fault. I must see the South of France, which
almost knocked me up, the heat was so intense,
particularly at Nismes and Avignon.' In the con-
cluding paragraph there is a sentence which strikes
one as characteristically casual: 'If you should be
passing Queen Anne Street, just say I am well and
in Rome,'—considering that, even omitting Hannah,
his father was still alive, and doubtless anxious
after two months' silence. Communication by proxy
saved him postage from the Continent, one must
suppose.

A clergyman who had been introduced to him in
London speaks of being his fellow-traveller in a diligence
at Macerata. His attention was first called to a 'funny

little elderly gentleman' who spoke only a few words
of Italian and French, and jumbled the two languages
together most amazingly, abusing the conductor for
not waiting long enough for him to sketch a sunrise.
"Damn the fellow!" he exclaimed aloud. "He has
no feeling!" The cleric, now recognising the
Academician, ventured to remind him of their previous
acquaintance, upon which Turner instantly became
deaf and dumb, pointedly turning his back. Upon
his being subsequently rallied for such churlishness,
he slyly remarked, with twinkling eyes, "How could
I presume to address so eminent a pillar of the
Church?"

Though presumably still a Member of the Roman
Academy of St. Luke, Turner hardly seems to have
been appreciated in the Eternal City. There was a
namesake of his there, a provision-merchant specialising in English comestibles, and the favourite quip
of the Roman art-critics was that one Turner sold
mustard and the other painted with it.

This, if you please, was when he was challenging
the very sun in its splendour, not only in the magnificent *Orvieto*, with its lovely distances beyond the
superbly rendered rays, but also making studies for
the unparalleled *Ulysses Deriding Polyphemus*, unquestionably his greatest work, and one of the outstanding
masterpieces of all time. It is as if Turner had at last
decided to show the world just what he could do when
he tried, and had determined that the picture should
include everything at which he particularly excelled.

The startling blaze of colour, uniquely daring in its contrasts, combines full sunlight and a fiery sunset. Handled with the utmost breadth and power, radiance mingles with gloom, and poetry with drama. It is indeed that oft-quoted 'magic casement' opening into wonderland. The magnificent portrayal of the giant alone makes the picture remarkable. The work has been disparaged as operatic, and belittled as inconsistent, incorrect, a madman's pipe-dream. So be it: the inspired visionary is never wholly sane, whether his name be Wagner, Blake, Turner, or St. John the Divine. The Apocalypse is by no means sane. But it is sublimely literature, just as *Ulysses* is sublimely Art, the final and victorious word in the imaginative interpretation of sheer beauty.

It was exhibited in 1829, and took the critics' breath away. In the previous year *Orvieto* had been thrown them as a sop 'to stop their gabbling', in Turner's own phrase. As a gesture of indifference, he railed a length of rope round it to form a frame.

In 1830, when William Hazlitt died and Christina Rossetti was born, Turner supplied twenty-five vignettes as illustrations to Samuel Rogers' "Italy", based on drawings made while on his recent tour there. They include some of his most delicate and highly-finished —occasionally too highly-finished—work, the very finest being, perhaps, *Jacqueline*, and *Alps at Daybreak*. Rogers was a successful banker as well as a minor poet, and, possibly for this reason, Turner made him an

Executor of his Will. The two men seem to have got on well, for we learn that they were often about together, Turner being also a frequent guest at the banker's house. That the hospitality was not returned is indicated by a caustic comment of Rogers when somebody admired a remarkable table in the painter's ante-room at Queen Anne Street. "How much more remarkable it would be," said Rogers, "to see any of his friends sitting round it!"

On Turner's credit side, however, it is told that when the *Italy* enterprise seemed shaky after £15,000 had been expended on it, he reduced his agreed fee of £50 per vignette, outright purchase, to £5 apiece for their serial use, the artist to retain the copyright. It is also undeniable that, in his illustrations to Rogers, Turner produced finer poems than Rogers was able to write.

He was in the company of Rogers at a village inn near London when a youth passed the window who was pointed out as Turner's natural son. The obvious inferences are that Turner was known in the locality, was not ashamed of his bastard, for whose upkeep he was presumably providing, since he did not avoid the district.

Apropos his illustrations to Rogers, and Scott, and Byron, it is well authenticated that he also made accompanying drawings to the works of Burns, Cowper, Campbell, Tennyson, Cervantes, and even Dickens. To Shakespeare as well, for there is a dramatic Romeo and Juliet painting dated 1824, and he likewise

158

portrayed Falstaff with Bardolph, the latter subject being admirably suited to the grossness of his figure-studies and his simple-minded humour.

This same year, 1830, the Academy exhibited various lesser paintings as well as *Orvieto*, painted 1828, and the output included *Chain Pier, Brighton*, and yet another view of Petworth Park. Hawkesworth Fawkes paid one of his periodical visits to Queen Anne Street, and, to please Turner, now fifty-five years old, brought with him the Rhenish drawings sold to the dead Squire of Farnley for £500. Turner looked through them eagerly, and when he came to *Twilight in the Lorelei*, his former favourite, his eyes filled with tears.

Another old friend passed away in 1830 in the P.R.A., Sir Thomas Lawrence. He was buried in St. Paul's, and the ground was covered with snow. As the black-clad pall-bearers passed, Turner murmured sadly, "Who will do the like for me?" to his neighbour, the tall, pale, quiet Sir David Wilkie, whose own funeral he was afterwards to immortalise in paint. Whimsical Scotch Wilkie, however, only had eyes for the colour contrasts of the dramatic scene, and, nudging Turner, whispered: "That's a fine effect." Turner is said to have turned away in disgust, thinking the remark in bad taste. But, as with so many other trains of thought started in his mind by other people, when he went home he noted down his recollection of the historic portico, and the sombre mourners moving up the snowy steps, adding touches of red as relief, and the result hangs in the National Gallery to-day. At Lawrence's sale he stopped one of his own drawings being sold, saying it was not the deceased's property, and had only been lent.

That unpleasant person, George IV, had died in the same year, having for some time past found it convenient to live in comparative seclusion, rather than court active public demonstrations of his unpopularity. So callously prodigal had he been of the nation's finances that his wardrobe alone realised £30,000; and no less than £10,000 in banknotes were discovered carelessly left in the pockets of his various suits. His successor, William IV, was described by Wellington as 'looking like a respectable old Admiral', and was remarkable for nothing but his vacillating timidity and futile, long-winded publicspeeches.

But a death now occurred which to Turner far outweighed that of any mere king. Old Father William's time had come, and in the last account we have of him he is chuckling with delighted pride because his "William painted the *Ulysses!*" His final resting-place was St. Paul's, Covent Garden, where he had been married and his famous son baptised. A monument was erected to him, but not until two years later, and the muddled wording upon it indicates that it was drafted by Turner himself.

TURNER IN MIDDLE-AGE
PORTRAIT DRAWING BY J. PHILLIP, R.A.
(*National Portrait Gallery*)

In the vault
Beneath and near this Place
are deposited the remains of
WILLIAM TURNER,
many years an inhabitant of this parish,
who died
September 21st, 1830
To his memory and of his wife,
MARY ANN,
Their son, J. M. W. Turner, R.A.,
has placed this Tablet,
August, 1832.

Turner was sincerely attached to his father, and the portrait-sketch he made of him in 1823 is affectionate and endearing. The loss of him, after so many years of intimate association, made a considerable difference to his existence. But when the churchwarden of St. Paul's ventured to present a bill for seven-and-six for mason's work in connection with the stone, Turner rushed away, directing the man to call at Queen Anne Street with a receipt, without which he would not pay. The churchwarden, after doing so several times fruitlessly, crossed off the small sum as a bad debt.

CHAPTER VIII

1831–8

FOR years previous to his father's death, the painter's superabundance of vitality had found an outlet, as we have seen, in occasional disappearances into the stews of Wapping; but these primitive debauches were, we can surmise, kept pretty dark, not only from a natural instinct of secrecy, but out of consideration for the feelings of the ex-barber, who had already had to stomach as best he might his son's relations with Hannah Danby. Once the old fellow was in his grave, however, not only must the artist, after so many years of close intimacy, have felt the need of new companionship, but also the convention of domesticity had thenceforward no more compelling call upon him than any other kind of tradition. It was in fact a demand of his pugnacious un-commonplace inner self to joy in flouting public opinion. How had the unimaginative helped *him?* And, since this is a human tale, and Turner above all other men was a connoisseur of beauty, perchance the mutilated face of Hannah Danby under that invariable big bonnet was not all-satisfying.

It is much more than probable, also, that the lady herself, left *tête-à-tête* at Queen Anne Street with an undeniable celebrity, became exigeant, demanding. For years she had had concrete proof not only of his distinguished position but of his increasing riches. The house was a veritable Tom Tiddler's Ground, for picking up gold and silver. Had it not been continually her duty to admit through that dingy door patrons who were Peers, Academicians whose names were household words, dealers and customers rolling in money, and all of them deferring to her master?

Hannah was a commonplace woman, and (except, perhaps, in her devotion to her mangy, tailless cats) a practical one. Considering that any newspaper she picked up was as likely as not to make some reference to the eccentric whose housekeeper and mistress she was, it is not surprising if she now thought of marriage, and of her prospective affluence when left a widow at not too far distant a date. After all, the guv'nor was a bachelor, and the undisputed father of her two young daughters, even though by mutual consent they were always referred to as her nieces. The fact that marriage was quite outside Turner's habits or intentions may not have occurred to her, but I doubt whether his grunted evasion of the proposition made life any easier in Queen Anne Street. If Hannah was the character we have reason to believe she was, she would not have taken *No* for an answer, and Turner's reaction would have been to vanish, to Wapping or elsewhere, anywhere in fact, till things had simmered down to normal.

Whatever the motive, the facts show that from now on Turner's parallel duplicate existence in the spirit and the flesh was to be so further complicated that he lived a double life in the most commonplace acceptance of the word. Under another name and in different surroundings he formed a new and lasting sexual connection, which appeared indefensible to Victorian moralists. While on this subject, it does strike the student of his life as somewhat ironical and unjust that though, with other successful followers of the various Arts, such as Titian, Wagner, da Vinci, Byron, George Sand, and Shelley, their liaisons could be winked at as romantic gallantries, in Turner's case any rumour of illicit sex-relation was sufficient to brand him as a depraved libertine. Perhaps it was because his amours were admittedly not picturesque; or possibly it was all part of the same class-hypocrisy which made the men-about-town of his time boast of being three-bottle-men, while looking askance at Turner's far more meagre jorum of sailor's rum or Academy brown sherry. It is difficult to pair up the legend of his chronic tipsiness with the complete absence in him at any time of what is modernly known as nerves (we hear of his remaining wholly imperturbable in spite of a salute of guns going off suddenly above his head) or with the undimmed eye which guided to pin-points of masterly effect the hand so steady that it never used a mahlstick.

Apropos also, he was never known to suffer from seasickness, though so much of his existence was spent upon the water in all weathers. After his father's death, we learn from a contemporary, he would travel down to his favourite Margate almost every Saturday morning by the 'Magnet' or 'King William' boat, looking like the skipper of some similar steamer. 'Most of the time he hung over the stern, watching the effects of the sun and the boiling of the foam.' And one may interpolate here that for a man, painter or otherwise, to have spent more than half a century, as he had done, in the constant study of nature is in itself not far from unique. 'About two o'clock,' we read, 'he would open his wallet of cold meat in the cabin, and, nearing himself to one with whom he was in the habit of chatting, he would beg a clean plate and a hot potato, and did not refuse one glass of wine, but would never accept two. It need hardly be added that he was no favourite with the waiters.'

Throughout his life the odd creature not only kept an elaborate diary, but in it entered meticulous accounts of his daily expenditure. An item which often recurs is 'Boxing Harry', signifying, in the commercial travellers' jargon of the time, what would now be known as High Tea, or a meat-tea, suggesting in any case that the thrifty creature was customarily satisfied with a mere snack at middle-day, a most unusual economy in those plenteous times, when all classes of the community did themselves abundantly well at table, as frequent passages in Dickens indicate. Possibly Turner had read, marked, learned, and inwardly digested the advice of the great Dr. Abernethy (who died just then, in 1831, the year of the publication of Lytton's 'Eugene Aram') that perfect health could be maintained by living on 6d. a day—and earning it.

In the diary and note-books he carried with him in addition to his sketch-books, he would add to his hasty drawings written comments, ungrammatical and ill-spelt, regarding effects to be secured later, just as on his uncompleted pictures (and on some completed ones) one may read hints of his intention in an almost illegible scrawl, such as 'sunshine', 'houses', 'yellowish-grey'.

Margate had always been so much to the artist's taste that, now for the first time a free agent, he decided to take up a more or less permanent abode there. This would account for the contemporary quoted above having seen him habitually on the week-end packet-boat. Near the Customs House he found a house advertising lodgings to let, and knocked at the door.

The woman who opened it to him was to be so identified with the remainder of his existence that she merits description. Turner kept their association so close a secret that it was not until more than twenty years later that any of his intimates got a glimpse of her. At that later period she was described as 'still a handsome woman' of about fifty, so that one may permissibly assume that when she opened the door of her lodging-house to Turner in 1831, she was, being then not yet thirty, definitely attractive. Of her type we learn from a not too sympathetic source that she was in those later years a 'big, hard, coarse, Scotch-woman', but that she when young instantly appealed to the fifty-six-year-old Turner is manifest from the immediate upshot, one of the quaintest and most characteristic episodes in all his strange story.

The landlady seems not to have 'tokened', as they say, to her prospective lodger; but his keenness was so great that he fumbled in his shapeless pocket, drew out a sheaf of dirty banknotes, and brandished them in the lady's face, offering to buy her house if she preferred it. The evidence of ready cash in bulk would have caused any landlady, let alone any Scots-woman, to hesitate.

"What's your name?" she temporised.

"What's yours?" demanded Turner.

"Mrs. Booth," returned the landlady.

"Then mine's *Mr*. Booth," declared Turner, and without further ado took up his abode in her house.

Nor was his answer mere repartee. From that time on he became Mr. Booth, and Mrs. Booth's spouse. Had she a legal husband already? I am inclined to suspect that she had, and I visualise a furtive, shifty-eyed deck-hand, usually away at sea, leaving his wife to fend for herself in the lodging-house, and complac-ently contented to be purblind, on receipts of grants from Turner. Whatever the complication, Mrs. Booth would from all accounts have been perfectly capable of handling it. She is subsequently described as 'over-shadowing Turner completely', and that she was a masterful personality is plain, inasmuch as the new Mr. Booth, unlike the slovenly J. M. W. Turner, became quite smart in his appearance. The woman was neat, her house was neat, and the master of the house had to be neat to suit. Strangely enough, the said master seems to have raised no objection. According to Dr. Price, another lodger in the house, who knew the odd pair throughout the whole of their connection, which lasted until Turner's death, the painter was quite docile when in Margate. He called the lady 'Old 'un', and she addressed him as 'Dear'. Out of his love for the sea, the new clothes he purchased were of maritime type, so conspicuously so that, round about the Customs House, and in the shore-side ale-houses he frequented, the disguised painter was rumoured to be a retired naval officer of distinction. One can picture Turner being tickled and flattered, and not denying the impeachment. Certain it is that before long, plain, lame, bandy-legged, sturdy, elderly Mr. Booth came to be known in Margate as Admiral Booth to all save the irreverent wharf-urchins, who referred to him as, variously, 'Puggy' Booth, and Mrs. Booth's 'Old Podgy'.

The Margate establishment continued in being for fifteen years to come. When Turner came to London, as he did most mid-weeks, or when travelling in the provinces and abroad, he shed both the naval clothes and genial tavern-haunting of Booth, and became his own untidy misogynist self. He was silent as the grave about his double life. Nobody, not even Hannah

Danby, seems to have suspected the existence of the 'Admiral' and his domestic hearth. The artist had never been in the habit of announcing his intended absences or explaining them on his return, and he did not alter now. He still used the Queen Anne Street gallery when he chose, but from this time on employed an agent called Griffith to keep in touch with customers and publishers. It is also most significant that soon after meeting Mrs. Booth he made his will, witnessed by a solicitor of Clement's Inn and two others, to which a codicil was added in the following year.

In 1831 the artist visited Scotland for the second series of illustrations to Sir Walter Scott earlier referred to. In the same year were exhibited *Fingal's Cave*, and *Caligula's Palace and Bridge*, the latter summarising, with *The Bay of Baiae* (1823), and *Childe Harold's Pilgrimage* (1832), the poet-painter's romantic visions of Italy, the lovely distances, picturesque ruins, luxuriant vegetation, and gay skies. The stage of progress is above all notable for his first pictures of Venice, an event of outstanding artistic importance, inasmuch as the dream-city figures in so many of his very greatest paintings, whether as subject, background, or inspiration.

Indeed, from now till 1846 there were only two years (1838–9) when the Academy did not exhibit Venice subjects from his brush, of which *Bridge of Sighs*, *Sun of Venice*, *Approach to Venice*, and *Evening, Going to the Ball*, must be particularly noted. It seems certain that the first few shown were worked up from sketches made at a former visit, the exact date of which is unknown. There is certainly nothing to indicate any trip abroad in the opening years of his Margate adventure. In his earlier paintings of 'The Queen of the Adriatic', the influence of Canaletto is strongly marked, but disappears as the painter ceases to be interested in the mere picturesqueness of canals and buildings, and instead re-discovers the city as an ideal aesthetic-platform for his projection of vivid colour-schemes, and, above all, of light. Gradually the material palaces give place to unreal fourth-dimensional glimpses of atmospheric magic, more and more chromatically daring, with beauty as the only touchstone. In Venice the seer came nearest to finding that rainbow he had for so many years strained to grasp.

Caligula's Palace, by the by, was handicapped by a quotation from "Fallacies of Hope".

> 'What now remains of all the mighty bridge
> Which made the Lucrine Lake an inner pool,
> Caligula, but massive fragments, left
> As monuments of doubt and ruined hopes
> Yet gleaming in the morning's ray, that tell
> How Baiae's shore was loved in times gone by?'

In 1832, the year of Sir Walter Scott's death, a forerunner to *Punch* was published, called *Punch in London*, under the editorship of Douglas Jerrold. In the following year, when slavery was abolished in

the British Colonies, and Brahms was born, Edmund
Kean died, as did also Dr. Monro, Turner's old friend
and patron. Turner, as was his way, attended the
subsequent auction to buy in his own works, securing
ninety early drawings for £80, and thus discovering
that the forgers were already at their pranks, several
lots vended being not by him at all. He was afterwards subpœnaed in a case respecting the authenticity
of one of his own works, and, much incensed, would
thereafter close up like an oyster when asked for a
decision.

In the same year the artist started his *Rivers of
France*. These sixty water-colours proved an instantaneous success, in spite of shortcomings already
mentioned, in spite, also, of the fatuous letterpress
accompanying them, by the author of "Dr. Syntax",
which latter even Rowlandson's uproarious vitality
was unable to save from oblivion. He was still perpetually at war with his engravers. One of them called
at Queen Anne Street to say that, rather than submit
to Turner's unfairness and extortions, he would put
the proofs he had brought with him on the fire. And,
angered by Turner's grin, he literally did so, and
for the first time penetrated the painter's insensibility.
Turner agitatedly rushed for the tongs to retrieve the
burning paper—but it was only because, as he never
went to the expense of having his chimneys swept,
he was afraid the house would be set on fire!

Work on the *Rivers* kept Turner busy till 1835,
red-letter years marked also by the births of Whistler

and William Morris, by Faraday's discovery of electric self-induction, the first publication of "The Last Days of Pompeii", and Carlyle's "Sartor Resartus", as well as the dramatic advent of Charles Dickens with his "Sketches by Boz", and the deaths of Coleridge, Charles Lamb, and Turner's old associate, Samuel Rogers.

In 1834, we must note in passing, Thomas Price Turner, the artist's cousin, came to London as a chorus singer in the Handel Festival, and, apparently learning for the first time that the painter was well known, decided to return the call paid on his father in Devonshire by Turner more than twenty years before. It is hardly surprising that he was not made particularly welcome, only, indeed, gaining admission at all at the third attempt, when, he subsequently complained, he was not even asked to sit down. This precious creature then ignored Turner for the remaining seventeen years of the painter's life, but on his death brought a law-suit laying claim to the whole of the artist's fortune and possessions.

The Rivers of France, apart from their outstanding beauty, proved very lucrative to Turner. It was primarily through the constant issue of similar series of engravings that he had by now already amassed the bulk of his huge fortune. We have already seen that he thought it no indignity for even a famous man to drive a hard bargain, and he invariably stipulated that he retained an interest in his works. One must remember, also, that, apart from his being

172

able for quite fifty years of his life to obtain high prices, the money went much farther because the ordinary commodities of existence were infinitely cheaper. And, in any case, Turner spent next to nothing, ever. But the major consideration to him of his present affluence, acquired by a lifetime of dogged perseverance and undeviating thrift, was that he was at last able to paint what and how and when and where he liked. His consequent independence gave him the reputation at this period of refusing all offers for the outright purchase of his work, whatever the price offered.

This, we learn, did not deter a certain Mr. Gillott, a Birmingham pen-manufacturer, from bearding the lion in his den. Hannah Danby, on opening the grimy door at Queen Anne Street to the prosperous-looking visitor, did not, we may be sure, place any undue obstacle upon the tradesman bursting unannounced into the Master's studio.

"I've come to buy some pictures," declared the unabashed interloper.

"'Aven't any to sell," grunted the old dog disturbed at his bone.

"Have you seen our Birmingham pictures?"

"Never even 'eard of 'em."

Gillott proceeded to lay on the table bank-notes to the tune of £5,000, and the artist's avaricious eyes, in spite of himself, began to glitter. Tempted, he still demurred, however.

"Mere paper," he mumbled, contemptuously.

"To be bartered for mere canvas," returned the unruffled manufacturer, indicating various dust-covered paintings which had caught his acquisitive glance, and which, after very little more parley, he carted away with him in the waiting cabriolet.

That Turner's queer humour appreciated the bourgeois' impudence is proved by a later incident when Gillott, having disposed of his £5,000's worth at a profit of three hundred per cent, came back for more. Turner amused himself by tempting the tradesman into higher and higher bids, with the object no doubt of discovering the true current market value. But at the end of the colloquy he had the last laugh, for, having worked the manufacturer into a frenzy of eagerness, he refused to part with a single further square inch of his work.

He was, as we have already seen, a great one at relishing a certain sort of joke. When his Academician friend, 'that fat fellow', Chantrey, pretended to warm his podgy hands at Turner's fiercely-coloured *Burning of the Two Houses of Parliament*, and, grinning all over his crimson face, enquired whether it had been painted to the commission of a Fire Insurance Company, Turner, far from being offended, burst out laughing, and chuckled simple-mindedly for days afterwards in recollection. It was this painting, by the by, of which Scarlett Davis, a talented, dissipated artist of the day, said: 'I have heard it spoken of as a failure—a devil of a lot of chrome. He finished it on the walls the last two days before the gallery opened to the public.

I am told it was good fun to see the great man whacking away with about fifty stupid apes standing round him, and I understand he was cursedly annoyed—the fools kept peeping into his colour box and examining all his brushes and colours.'

This year, 1835, in which his *Grand Canal, Venice*, was also shown for the first time, was afterwards estimated by Ruskin to mark the beginning of Turner's Third and Last Period. In 1835 Ruskin was only sixteen, and had his first glimpse of Turner's actual work in the shape of a number of water-colours of various periods in a private collection. Hitherto he had only known his name and art through the illustrations to Rogers' "Italy", given him when a schoolboy by his father. It was owing to the precocious critic's advice that the father, a rich wine-merchant, now began to add Turner to his collection of pictures. When, in the following year, the painter's Academy exhibits, *Juliet and her Nurse*, *Rome from Mount Aventine*, and *Mercury and Argus*, were attacked in the Press, more especially in Blackwood's, Ruskin, by now an undergraduate of Christ Church, Oxford, wrote an essay strongly protesting, and enthusiastically defending the sixty-one-year-old artist. The article was never published because it was first submitted to Turner, who signified his disapproval in the phrase: "I never move in these matters." Indeed, at no time, then or afterwards, was the externally matter-of-fact painter anything but uncomfortable in the face of Ruskin's lyrical rhapsodies of his work.

"He knows a great deal more about my pictures than I do," was his sardonic dictum. "He puts things into my head, and points out meanings in them, that I never intended."

The fact is that Ruskin set on paper the emotions aroused in his own hectic temperament, instead of analysing the art-work that inspired them. Dickens was simultaneously being carried away by other wild enthusiasms and animosities, and voicing them in the same perfervid fashion. It was a letting-off of steam peculiar to the epoch. The incident cited above nevertheless marked the first connection between Turner and his destined partisan.

The journals which were so hostile to Turner that year give us other items of interest—the publication of "Pickwick", and Disraeli's "Henrietta Temple", the death of Macadam (of Macadamised roads) and, in theatrical news, the appearance of Mme. Malibran in Balfe's brand-new opera "The Maid of Artois", the retirement of Charles Kemble, and the death of George Colman the Younger, who in his adventurous life had married an actress at Gretna Green, resided for years in the King's Bench prison, and written many highly-censorable comedies, until he was appointed Censor of Plays, after which he became unduly censorious of other dramatists' work, like Charles Brookfield some three-quarters of a century later.

Turner's wealthy patron, Munro of Novar (not to be confused with the 'good Doctor' Monro, of Adelphi Terrace), now suggested that they should together take a sketching tour in France and Switzerland, concerning which a number of characteristic anecdotes are happily preserved. Munro seems to have been surprised that Turner never vouchsafed in words any enthusiasm for the beauty-spots they visited. But he insists that in spite of Turner allowing himself no cessation from labour *en route*, he nevertheless enjoyed himself in his 'honest Diogenes' fashion, adding significantly 'if you bore with his way'. He was apt, as ever, to be peevish when questioned about his methods of work; used spittle to moisten his powder-colours, preferred his all-but-hairless brushes for sky-effects, and had a horror of being 'too mappy' in his distances. He preferred not to work side by side with his companion, but made rapid sketches which he would complete at their inn of an evening.

We learn of Munro being disheartened with his own efforts, and Turner demanding "What are you in search of?" and of his saying, when Munro had failed in an effect, "You should take subjects more suited to your capacity." But we also hear, in softer vein, of the Master taking away a block-book of Munro's, disappearing without explanation, then returning it with the grumble: "I can make nothing of *your* paper." But on the block in the meantime he had made three process sketches of the same view —the Pont St. Martin—in graduated stages of progress, to indicate in the clearest fashion to his patron-pupil how the amateur's difficulties could be overcome.

He detested to be thought kind, and had no objection to seeming the opposite. It was on this same Continental tour that Munro commissioned from him a certain view of Rome. The picture, unusually punctilious in point of topographical accuracy, was so painted to please his patron, and at that period of Turner's life was virtually beyond price. He refused, however, to accept more than £300 for it, on the grounds that Munro had paid him just that sum for previous, similar, commissions.

The purchaser was sufficiently appreciative of his good fortune to order a companion-picture of Venice. Turner went there specially, returned and delivered the picture, but, when the customary £300 was proffered, insisted on his expenses in addition. The incident has been widely quoted as an example of the painter's meanness; but for my part, even while grinning, I am inclined to think there is another side to the question. That Turner had 'spoiled' the naughty child Munro of Novar is pretty evident when we learn that Munro, huffed by the expenses incident, got rid of his £300 *Venice* purchase—for £3,000!

A life-long friend of Turner's, Wells, the drawing-master, died in this year; and his daughter describes how, when the news reached him of his old friend's end, Turner came immediately to the house, and there sobbed unrestrainedly.

"Oh, Clara, Clara! these are iron tears! I have lost the best friend I ever had!" he reiterated, so she tells us; and then went on to remind her of all their happy times together—of how as a young girl she used to read aloud while her father and he sketched by lamplight, and of his family-rompings with her younger sisters, when they drove him like a horse with his cravat for reins.

When it was found that the widow had been left unprovided for, he insisted upon lending her money, and continued over so long a period that a substantial sum was owing. A capable woman, she eventually found her feet, and with rare honesty and gratitude came to repay the whole debt to Turner. He, however, put his hands in his pockets, projecting his obstinate jaw.

"Keep it," he said, "and send your children to school and to Church."

Yes: I think it must be admitted that the complex Turner had the simple instinct for friendship, curmudgeon or no. Apart from Wells, and Fawkes, and Lord Egremont, Girtin in earlier years, and the Ruskins, father and son, later on—apart from his father, one might add—and all his low-life cronies in Wapping, Deptford, and at Margate, his brother-Academicians were devoted to him, not only as whole-hearted admirers of his art (Constable, for instance, affirmed that it was the most complete work of genius known to him, and asked: "Did you ever see a picture by Turner and not wish to possess it?') but in affection for the man himself. During Turner's increasingly frequent and unexplained absences from Queen Anne Street and the Academy meetings,

Chantrey and his fellows evinced the greatest concern for their colleague's health and safety, and always greeted his reappearance with enthusiasm and relief. In his rare correspondence also, we find that gifts of game and other dainties were habitually sent him, not only from Farnley, but by other friends.

The mere chronology of his work at this period indicates that Admiral Puggy Booth was spending longer and longer periods at Margate. If Hannah Danby was proving restive at her unlawful spouse's disinclination to make an honest woman of her and legitimatise her children, she certainly made no effort to render the Queen Anne Street house a more attractive abode, for we read that at this period it was more dilapidated than ever, with the oiled paper from the 'Turner Gallery' skylight hanging in sooty strips, and the damp entering, to the detriment of the art-works hung and heaped haphazardly about the walls, rotting for want of care, and merely providing hiding-places for the housekeeper's mangy cats.

But, however thick the dust and mildew, there stood always on the ramshackle sideboard, beside the discarded flute and music, the artist's hospitable sherry in its cracked decanter beside the single dirty glass. One can only surmise that his own supplies were closeted elsewhere, or possibly he kept his potations for after working-hours and the tavern— where, we learn, he was wont to add, now a little brandy, now a little water, to a never-empty glass until the bottle and the evening were ended.

We also find, somewhat surprisingly, that at this period he occasionally played cards for money. But his visits to town were rare. Not only was his energy naturally diminishing with the years, but, apart from there no longer being any financial necessity for him to work when he did not feel so disposed, Admiral Booth had by this time two growing children in Margate to enliven his declining years, in addition to Hannah Danby's two 'nieces' in London.

Consequently, in the years 1837–8 there is little output or professional activity to record beyond another Venice subject, *The Marriage of the Adriatic*, and the fact that Turner bought in for £3,000 his own *England and Wales* series, and refused to re-sell the plates either piece-meal or as a whole. When Bohn, the publisher, offered to pay an equal sum for the printed stock alone, Turner made a breakfast appointment for the next day to clinch the matter—by which time, however, he had conveniently forgotten the whole transaction.

But, though Turner was resting on his oars, the great world was vigorously spinning around him. 1066 apart, 1837 is the only date in English history most people can remember, as marking the accession of Queen Victoria, and of her 'promise to be good'. Her predecessor, the feeble, garrulous, and irascible William IV, had died on June 20th, less than a month after Victoria had ceased to be legally a Minor. He died happy, however, for he detested the young Princess's mother, the Duchess of Kent, and had fought hard through his last illness to live just long enough to prevent the Duchess becoming Regent. Other things were happening. Constable died and Carlyle's "French Revolution" appeared, as did the first parts of "Oliver Twist", to be followed by "Nicholas Nickleby" in the following year, 1838, when the National Gallery was opened, the first steamer crossed the Atlantic, and Paganini sent Berlioz 20,000 francs for his "Harold in Italy".

CHAPTER IX

1839-45

SOME connoisseurs, other than Ruskin, consider that 1840, and not 1835, marked the commencement of Turner's Last Period, and it is arguable that it was also his finest. It is indisputable that his output during it is entirely unimitative. The new era opened with the production of the most generally popular and frequently reproduced of all his works, '*Old Téméraire*' *Being Towed to Her Last Moorings*. It was also the artist's own favourite among all his pictures, and when empowering the Executors of his will to select a painting each as a memento, he excluded the *Téméraire*. Though not accepted by critics as his greatest masterpiece, it is utterly English, it deftly links his most characteristic qualities, and is beyond question one of the finest and most celebrated pictures in the world. The first notion was given Turner when steaming down the Thames with a party of brother-Academicians to take whitebait at Greenwich. An old battleship, condemned in August 1838 after doughty work in the battles of Trafalgar and the Nile, was being tugged to Deptford, there to become an international hospital-hulk for sailors. Clarkson Stanfield, seeing Turner's watchful eye upon it, suggested it would make a fine subject for him.

Turner's first title for the completed work was *The Fighting 'Téméraire'*, the name by which it is commonly known. John Martin, a contemporary, and himself an artist, speaks of visiting Queen Anne Street, and finding the Master actually engaged upon the picture.

'We found the great painter at work upon his well-known picture, *The Fighting 'Téméraire'*. Mr. Turner hardly struck one as a man who was producing works so full of poetry and art. His dress was certainly not that of a refined gentleman and painter. A loose body coat, very open side pockets, with a dirty paint rag stuck in one of them; loose trousers, unbraced, and hanging under the heels of his slippers; a large rosewood palette with a very big bunch of brushes of various sizes in his hand, and a rather old hat on his head—such was J. M. W. Turner at work. The studio was dark and gloomy, in every way like that of an untidy man, and not at all what one would have expected from so great a painter.'

Martin further adds, regarding Queen Anne Street, that the only visitors, except for chance calls like the above, 'were those of patrons or connected with professional requirements. No members of the fair sex were ever seen to enter the house. In person, not only in his study, but at all times, Turner was untidy; a sloven and unwashed—one that might well have been taken for a Hebrew 'Old Clo' dealer, but certainly not for the greatest poetical landscape painter of his age!'

Of all his brilliant colour challenges the *Téméraire* is the most striking. On Varnishing Day in the Academy of 1839 it was hung below a portrait-study by Geddes, A.R.A., who, observing that the gorgeous sunset in Turner's picture killed his own work, hastily proceeded to add a bright red carpet to his *A Lady and Children* hanging above. Turner, however, saw it in time, and crying "Oho, Mr. Geddes!" intensified the splendour of his own sea-piece by laying on scarlet, orange, yellow, with a palette-knife.

Such was his certainty of touch, acquired by long years of labour and experience, that he would send in to the Exhibitions the merest sketch on canvas, and complete the work during the four Varnishing Days, arriving at six in the morning or even earlier, and staying till late at night, until the masterpiece had fully come to being. This habit was naturally dreaded by his fellow-craftsmen, particularly the rival landscape-artists, towards whose work he was quite ruthless.

In order to obtain an effective chromatic contrast to his pictures, he once went to the unheard-of length of offering to pay for the re-upholstering of the seats in the Academy Exhibition Gallery, provided he chose the material. Chantry and his colleagues thought it was one of the eccentric's occasional impulses of generosity; but their eyes were opened when they saw the new scarlet covers, selected to act as a dazzling foil to the donor's colour-schemes.

C. R. Leslie, an Associate of the time, speaks of the

informal Academician's lunches which lightened Varnishing Days. Turner, it appears, was the life and soul of the table, and it was he, the proverbially unconvivial, who said, when it was suggested such functions should be abolished: "Then you will do away with the only social meetings we have, the only occasion on which we all come together in an easy, unrestrained manner."

Wilkie Collins, as a boy, remembers seeing Turner on such Varnishing Days 'seated on the top of a flight of steps astride a box (not the more perfect in his balance for the brown sherry at the Academy lunch). There he sat, a shabby Bacchus, nodding like a Mandarin at his picture, which he, with a pendulum motion, now touched with his brush and now receded from. Yet, in spite of sherry, precarious seat, and old age, he went on shaping in some wonderful dream of colour, every touch meaning something, every pin's head of colour being a note in the chromatic scale.'

It is one of the most amazing things about the whole of his *œuvre* in maturity that what appear to be, viewed closely, mere casual dots and dashes, tell, when seen from a proper distance, as rows of houses, a winding stream, meadows, rockets (as in *Burial At Sea*), or exquisite cloud effects.

The pathos of the *Téméraire's* subject as well as its masterly treatment brought an immediate success for the picture, though many critics since then have picked it to pieces upon a number of counts, principally

186

that the man-o'-war bears as little resemblance
to Nelson's sturdy battleship as does the tug to
any actual craft; and that the lighting is inconsistent, not to say impossible. To which Turner
would undoubtedly have replied, "What does it
matter? The effect is there". An early visitor to the
Exhibition was so enthralled that he rushed round
to Queen Anne Street and asked Turner to name
his own figure, but the artist, after mumbling
quaintly and characteristically, that it was his
'usual 200 guineas size", declined to sell at any
price, having doubtless already decided to bequeath
it to the nation.

According to Ruskin, this sunset theme marks the
close of Turner's greatest period, which had commenced with the sunrise of the *Ulysses*. Though I
shall venture to differ here, as on many other points,
with the critic, it is necessary to record his dictum,
inasmuch as Ruskin's young life became from this
time on indelibly associated with Turner's declining
one. With his *Téméraire* Turner was once again the
victim of an uncomprehending Press. Even to the
admirers of his earlier pictures, it appeared grotesque,
exaggerated, and even insane. The artist, like Whistler
later on, was accused of 'flinging a pot of paint in
the public's face', and the masterpiece earned him not
only abuse but ridicule. The lampooners included
Thackeray, who ought to have known better, having
himself studied art both in London and Paris. Possibly
the fact that he had just been rejected by Dickens as

an illustrator of his works made him bitter; or, alternatively, the work of Turner, a common man and the son of a barber, could *ipso facto* have no appeal for that Old Carthusian and arch-snob, the author of "The Book of Snobs".

Into this wordy warfare plunged the enthusiastic Ruskin, who from now on was to be the painter's doughtiest champion. It is said that the young critic had only just recovered from an abortive love-affair, and that Turner merely happened along as a new peg on which to hang his rhapsodies. Whatever the reason I am compelled to admit that the universal acceptance of Turner as a supreme genius was principally due to Ruskin's overstrained word-pictures. Just as that Victorianly-festooned prose leaves me merely inimical, so my studies of the author himself, particularly in his subsequent relations with the Rossettis, breed active dislike. He strikes me as an emasculate and pretentious windbag, and I cannot forget that while professing a sort of gentlemanly Fabianesque socialism, and declaring that tuition in the appreciation of Art ought to be put within reach of the masses, he was careful to arrange that his own works on the subject should continue to be published at prices prohibitive to the ordinary purse.

My distaste for the man as well as the writer was apparently shared by Turner, on whom, we learn, the critic by no means made a favourable impression at their first actual meeting in 1840. The painter, however, was no fool: and it must have been evident to him that the self-confident young fellow already had the ear of the public, and that his opinions were likely to become more and more generally received. There was no point in quarrelling with him, even apart from the fact of his rich wine-merchant father being an ardent picture-collector. It must not surprise us, therefore, to find later that the old artist broke through his unsociable habits sufficiently to dine pretty regularly with the Ruskins at their mansion on Denmark Hill.

In 1839, the year of the Chartist Riots, when Horace Smith died, and Lytton's two famous plays "The Lady of Lyons" and "Richelieu", were first produced, Turner paid his last visit to Rome, and the world was the gainer in his *Tivoli* and *Arch of Constantine*.

He also toured in Switzerland in this same year, and wrote facetiously to his colleagues at home, calling himself Mr. Avalanche Jenkinson. His itinerant diary is extant, elaborate and illiterate as ever, but space permits only a few highly characteristic extracts

'May 16th: Poligny a dirty town at the foot of the Jura, we were detained here a day from heavy rain—no setting room, meals in my bedroom large looking on the Square; French troops (on their way to Africa) drinking at the fountain——"

An expenses-note follows, with an F standing for Francs and an S presumably for Centimes!

	F.	S.
Posting	71	10
Passport	1	—
Bill	53	—

Later he is in Lausanne, 'a fatiguing town to walk in deep vallies', with 'groupes of women washing vegetables'; and at Signau we read, 'Landlord spoke only German, we made signs for our dinner'.

Perhaps this was the same landlord who, upon being interrogated by a visitor who had noticed Turner's name in the Hotel Register, described him thus—'A rough clumsy man, and you may know him by his always having a pencil in his hand', adding that his painting-materials were not worth half a crown. It was during this tour that his companion, a brother-artist, complained of having failed to obtain the effect he had tried for in a view of Domodossola which had intrigued him in the past, but which, when he went back again, 'looked so different' from how he had imagined it.

"What!" cried Turner in surprise. "Do you not know yet, at your age, that you ought to paint your impressions?"

1840 brought the artist's striking *Evening Star*, the same year that saw Queen Victoria married to Prince Albert, the introduction of the Penny Post, and the removal of Napoleon Buonaparte's remains to his magnificent last resting -place in Paris. Notable deaths included Fanny Burney and 'Beau' Brummel, the latter in a pauper lunatic-asylum, after his having once been *persona grata* with the highest in the land.

In the same year the 'Fallacies of Hope ' bobs up again with the following caption to his *Slavers Throwing Overboard the Dead and Dying* :—

> 'Aloft all hands, strike the topmasts and belay;
> Yon angry setting sun and fierce-edged clouds
> Declare the Typhoon's coming.
> Before it sweeps your decks throw overboard
> The dead and dying—ne'er heed their claims.
> Hope, Hope, fallacious Hope!
> Where is thy market now?'

The picture was not much better than the verse, unfortunately. A nightmare of dead and dying, sharks and chains and cormorants, it definitely marks decline of power. Perhaps because it formed the subject of a rhapsodical eulogy by Ruskin, a painter from America (to which country the picture was sold) designated it 'one of the most infernal pieces of clap-trap ever painted'.

1840 also brought us the well-known portrait of Turner by William Parrott called *Varnishing Day*, the original of which is in the Ruskin Museum at Sheffield. Taken surreptitiously while he was at work, it gives us the short and podgy figure, the 'Old Clo' hat and coat, with its paint-bag in the pocket, and the nose close up against the canvas with which we are already familiar. All through his life there were artists who made rapid sketches of him unawares, for he was of course the last person to be induced to pose. So we get, apart from the youthful portraits by Dance and Turner himself, already referred to, the impression that he variously made upon his amateur friends Fawkes and Munro of Novar, as well as upon Mulready, Sir John Gilbert (a convincing water-colour in old age), Charles Turner, the mezzotint engraver of his *Liber Studiorum*, upon J. Phillip, R.A., (reproduced in this volume); and, in the last year of his life, Count D'Orsay. Including his own self-sketch in 1823, all agree as to 'the little, bowlegged, snuffy, big-headed man with the small hands and feet' described by Haldane Macfall, but his homeliness, stockiness, podginess, lameness, red weather-beaten face, parrot's nose, staring beady eyes and *dirty* hands also emerge, as well as his occasional tendency to garish finery, like Goldsmith, evidenced in the Linnell picture. This shows a swagger coat with velvet collar, red waistcoat, and coral pin in the voluminous black satin stock. Surveying the National Portrait Gallery likeness by Phillip, one can appreciate how the customary epithets, 'Jew' and 'curmudgeon', came to be applied, but there is discernible also his dour humour, seeing eye, and the sensibility one would expect. Landseer also did a small sketch-portrait in oils one Varnishing Day, but gave it to a brother-artist who took it home in his top-hat, smudging it irretrievably. In D'Orsay's dilettante sketch he is depicted at an evening party, grimly sipping his tea by a piano, an old, old man in ill-fitting dress-tails, frilled shirt, and dancing-pumps.

But I anticipate, by a decade. The year is 1841, when Livingstone discovered Lake Ngami, Edward VII was born, and Punch first appeared, under the editorship of Mark Lemon and Horace Mayhew. Literature was the richer that year by the first issue of Harrison Ainsworth's "Guy Fawkes" and "Old St. Paul's", Poe's "Tales of Mystery and Imagination", and Dickens' "Old Curiosity Shop" and "Barnaby Rudge"; but the poorer by the death of Theodore Hook.

The death that more nearly affected Turner, however, was that of his old crony, Sir Francis Chantrey. In every instance that has come down to us of his friends passing, it seems to have been to him not only a tremendous shock but equally a surprise. In these later years the dread of his own death weighed heavily upon him, as perhaps is natural when a man sees his contemporaries one by one disappear. In the instance of Chantrey, who had that same year bought Turner's *Ducal Palace* on Varnishing Day, Turner, hastening to the house of mourning in Eccleston Street, found that George Jones had preceded him. Grasping Jones' hand, he stood weeping silently, and finally bolted from the house without uttering a word.

In the Chantrey Sale the *Ducal Palace*, for which Turner had received £250, realised £1,500. At about the same time fifteen of the artist's water-colours were sold by him for eighty guineas apiece, though one example alone subsequently fetched a thousand pounds.

In the following year another comrade, Sir David Wilkie, died in a steamer while returning from the East, and was buried off Gibraltar. This whimsical Scotsman, a confirmed bachelor, had been a rival as well as an associate of Turner, but with his passing all differences were forgotten. As a lasting memorial to his dead friend, Turner painted his intensely-characteristic *Peace—Burial at Sea*, striking the note of grief by painting the sails of the vessel quite black. Too black, considered Clarkson Stanfield, but Turner's grim comment was: "I only wish I had any colour to make them blacker."

Turner's powers were now generally considered to be waning. His eyesight was impaired, and, though his hand was still so steady that he had no need to use a mahlstick, he was subject to the imputation that his work was done under the influence of liquor. Genius is always lonely, and his solitariness of spirit now seems to have commenced to weigh upon him. He is spoken of as frequenting The Yorkshire Stingo, and of having been incoherently voluble at Offley's in Henrietta Street, on the subject of the scenery in a Shakespearian production at Drury Lane. He appears also to have had a liking for the Athenaeum Club, because they stocked a special brand of sherry. If, as alleged, he was wont to wax loquaciously maudlin in those austere

194

years. "Soapsuds and whitewash!" he repeated sadly for days after the attack. "What do they think the sea's like?"

And now one can describe with joy just how this enthusiast of sixty-seven was able to canvas for posterity in the immortal *Snowstorm* atmospheric effects never attempted by any other artist. Let me give the full title:——*Snowstorm—Steamboat off a Harbour's Mouth Making Signals in Shallow Water and Going by the Lead. The Author was in this Storm on the Night the Ariel Left Harwich.*

Yea, verily: the author was in that storm. At sixty-seven he made the sailors lash him to the mast in order to observe it. Hear his own words—"I did not paint it to be understood, but I wished to show what such a scene was like. I was lashed for four hours, and I did not expect to escape; but I felt bound to record it if I did." Soapsuds and whitewash indeed!

Unbiased critics find no sign of waning power in *Snowstorm*, or *The Splugen* ('the best Swiss landscape yet painted by man', according to Ruskin), any more than in the startling works of genius in the following year. *The Sun of Venice*, *The Morning After the Deluge*, and particularly *The Approach to Venice*, which, though the most sublime of all his Venice pictures, once again roused storms of adverse comment, and strangely enough seems to have been bewilderingly incomprehensible to his warmest supporters. The insinuations as to his insanity were re-doubled, the main charge against him being that he painted only what other

people could not see—a charge that Turner himself
would have been contented to accept as epitaph.
It is true that he was attempting more than ever
to pin down on to canvas the utterly intangible, but
it seems not to have occurred to his contemporaries
to ignore his intentions and accept what he gave them
at its face value, visions of unimaginable splendour,
beauty, and delight. His detractors adduced as further
proofs of madness his misanthropy and preference for
squalid surroundings. That he in time became at
least partly deranged it is idle to deny; that he was
queer in his head through all his life might reasonably
be argued, but it was only the dementia of some petty
farmer who has brooded on imaginary grievances,
it was only the mania of Turner's own mother, the
blame for whose insanity could never be ascribed to
Art. Little-mindedness, an undeniable characteristic
of Turner's crasser self, is obviously next door to no-
mindedness. Fortunately for himself and posterity,
however, there was always another unseen world of
revelations in which his unfettered spirit could magically soar.

Now, however, as an antidote to ignorant outcry,
appeared the first volume of Ruskin's "Modern
Painters", which, with all its rhodomontade, wrong-
headedness and false conclusions, undoubtedly made
not only the author's reputation, but also art-history.
Though called "Modern Painters" it was, in fact,
about one modern painter only, Turner, and his
pre-eminence over all others, dead or alive, and more

particularly over Claude, the Dutch Masters, and Poussin. One notes with some amusement that Turner was, in his own words, "fretted" by its publication, and could not be induced to read a word of it or any subsequent work of the author's. It is surely somewhat more than a coincidence, however, that, upon its instantaneous success, Turner was offered by Munro of Novar the enormous sum of £25,000 (or £87,500 to-day) for the contents of his Queen Anne Street gallery. With "soapsuds and whitewash" doubtless still ringing in his ears, he refused, and in characteristic fashion.

"No! I won't—I can't," he mumbled. "Besides . . . I can't be bothered. Good evening."

He couldn't be bothered, this eccentric who had already decided to leave all his work and fortune to the nation, this shy odd creature who was seen on the Margate packet that same year, delighting in the squall, and eating shrimps from a red pocket-handkerchief.

Was he already a little touched in the head, as his detractors suggested? Maybe. An incident of the same year seems to indicate it. This was the period of early experiments in photography, and Mayall, the inventor, tells of a bow-legged, lame, beak-nosed, podgy, shabby little fellow coming to him with an offer of finance. Mayall recognised the celebrated oddity immediately, but his visitor forestalled him by announcing that he was (of all weird things) a Master in Chancery! It is interesting enough that Turner, who in his youth had forestalled photography by touring, making commissioned views of noblemen's estates, should be among the first to appreciate the commercial possibilities of the inventor; but the Master in Chancery complication is surely even more intriguing. Why Master in Chancery? Mayall puts it down to his visitor having a screw loose, but I myself seem to perceive in it a sort of rebound from Admiral Booth—that constitutional secretiveness, of course, plus the advantage of anonymity when about to drive a bargain, plus, I feel sure, a childish love of dressing-up, as it were.

In 1843, when Mme. Patti was born, Turner exhibited *The Opening of the Walhalla*, with the following excerpt from the "Fallacies":—

' Who rode on thy relentless car, fallacious Hope?
He, though scathed at Ratisbon, poured on
The tide of war o'er all thy plain, Bavare,
Like the swollen Danube to the gates of Wien;
  But peace returns—the morning ray
Beams on the Walhalla, reared to science and the
    arts,
And men renowned, of German fatherland.'

The picture was dedicated to the King of Bavaria, to whom Turner sent it as a free gift. The monarch returned it, frankly confessing he was unable to understand it—nor the poetry either, perhaps! In that year, extending over into 1844, the painter visited the continent for the last time, an extended tour, disturbing his intimates greatly, since he neglected to inform them of his movements or the probable date of his return. He shifted, we learn, haphazardly from one *milieu* to another, avoiding his countrymen, a lonely, wistful, disillusioned patriarch; but was back in time for young Ruskin's birthday-party at Denmark Hill, a social engagement he kept yearly from this time on until his death. As usual, his portfolio was full, not only with fifteen water-colours destined to be famous, but hundreds of sketches which he had made round Heidelberg, Lucerne, Thun, Interlaken, Grundelwald and elsewhere. One notable painting, also, this tour produced—*Fishing Boats bringing a Disabled Ship into Port Ruysdael*, which conveys to some an indication of the physical helplessness the painter had so much come to dread, and which was intensified by the death of his friend Callcott.

And yet that his indomitable spirit was still marching on is revealed by the fact that in this, his seventieth year, he twice tried to tramp across the Alps, and only on his second failure said: "I confess the rigours of winter begin to tell on me."

Yet how in common justice can any diminution of ability be discerned in his masterly *Rain, Steam, and Speed*, dated this same year? Dickens, with his "Martin Chuzzlewit" and Disraeli with Coninsgby were repeating their tried formulae of success, but Turner's picture, which hangs in Trafalgar Square for all to see, flies out at one in its unprecedented originality and daring.

If ever there was *action* in a picture it is in this one: the modern French critic who on seeing it murmured "Impressioniste!" had hit the truth respecting a work so arresting as to make the poetic Mallarmé acclaim its author as 'the greatest painter that has ever lived'. 'Indistinct,' the critics called it! To which Turner's grinning reply was: "Indistinctness is my forte!"

Throughout the Master's story we have seen him opening new windows in Art, and here, at seventy, was yet another. Nor was it to be the last. In the few years yet remaining to him he was to give us other imperishable masterpieces, brought into being in a new environment, which formed the background of the last phase of his strange existence. Queen Anne Street was hardly to see him again, save as a corpse lying in state. And so, before we move on, let us wind up the present skein with a visit at 1 a.m. by Ruskin to the gloomy 'Turner Gallery' behind that dingy door. The accumulated grime of forty years lay over huge boxes containing, it was subsequently reckoned, £25,000 worth of drawings, sketches, proofs, and prints. In the mildewed drawing-room alone were stacked against the wall, unframed, not less than £80,000 work of paintings, complete and incomplete. The glazed top of the gallery was a mass of patches, barely weatherproof. It was clear that no window was ever opened. The corners of the studio were occupied with huge rolled canvases like dirty shrouds, and the whole was lit by the end of a tallow candle stuck in a bottle.

Covered with dust on the rickety dresser was the same old cracked decanter with its solitary unwashed wine-glass.

"'Ave a glass of sherry, now you're 'ere," the host urged Ruskin.

"It's really excellent sherry," declared the wine-merchant's son, sipping.

"It ought to be," chuckled Turner. "It's bin standing there since you were 'ere a year ago."

CHAPTER X

1845-51

IN 1845 Turner's eyesight was definitely failing, and with it equally his mind and powers. His subsequent pictures, with the few notable exceptions already foreshadowed, have on them all the marks of decay. The artist was a broken man, and, though terrified of death, reluctant to recognise its approach. The passing, not only of his friends, but of public men like Tom Hood and "Ingoldsby Legends" Barham, weighed with increasing heaviness upon him, and he was heard more than once to say that he would willingly have exchanged all his fame and riches to be twenty again.

The critics did not hesitate to kick the man when he was down, and even more merrily than heretofore 'blackened their mothers' milk to make printer's ink', to use Shaw's pungent, Swift-like phrase. Their ridicule deeply wounded the hyper-sensitive artist. "A man may be weak in his old age," he protested sadly, "but you should not tell him so." He practised what he preached, moreover, for Ruskin records that '. . . during the period of his life when the brightest qualities of his mind were, in many respects, diminished, and when he was suffering most from the evil speaking of the world, I never heard him say one depreciating word of living man or man's work, or pass, without some endeavour at mitigation, a blameful word spoken of another. Of no man, but Turner, whom I have ever known could I say this.'

He seems to have wished only to creep away and die, and now began, there seems little doubt, to seek in Dr. Johnson's words, 'to forget the pain of existence in unconvivial potations'. His declining health rendered the journeys between London and Margate too much for him, and this fact, it is abundantly clear to me, caused the masterful Mrs. Booth to intervene with such effect that the world is the richer for a number of other paintings, of surpassing power and beauty. Granted his career and life were drawing to a close, she seems to have argued, and granted that Margate was no longer possible, he could still with his ample means be Admiral Booth instead of a celebrated painter, could still pass the remainder of his days in ease and comfort by his beloved waterside, but in London, in some riverside quarter where none of his artistic friends would be liable to find him.

Though, as always, he kept his plans a secret, we have well-authenticated accounts of the immediate upshot. Cremorne Gardens, near where the Lots Road Power-station now stands, in Chelsea, was at that time a popular place of entertainment (Jos. Sedley found it so in "Vanity Fair") and thus remained till 1877. A small property owner on the wharf near by describes how in 1845 an elderly odd couple, the woman tall and gaunt and manifestly illiterate, the

205

man short, with a beaky nose, applied to him for the occupation of Cremorne Cottage, situated at 119 Cheyne Walk, and looking out westwards over that part of the Thames afterwards also immortalised by Whistler. The terms were agreed, but negotiations fell through owing to the disinclination of the would-be tenants to supply him either with their name or references. Subsequently the strangers returned, the man proffering in lieu of references any amount of money the landlord felt would guarantee him against risk. The offer was accepted, for the cottage was in bad repair, and the owner had had difficulty in letting it, and the lease was signed in the name of Sophia Caroline Booth.

Henceforward the little parrot-nosed old character, limping along in his semi-naval garb, was to be a familiar sight about Cremorne and Chelsea generally. The name of 'Admiral' and even 'Puggy' had followed him from Margate, doubtless revealed by himself with alcoholic chuckles in the neighbouring King's Arms, which he frequented, and where he had the reputation of being a retired mariner, fallen on bad times, and given to drink, but of kindly if eccentric disposition. Turner seems, indeed, to have been far happier in this environment than he ever was in his proper sphere among his brother Academicians, or as an honoured guest at Farnley Hall or with Lord Egremont at Petworth.

Mrs. Booth similarly appears to have been in her element. Under her vigorous influence the shabby, narrow-staired cottage was turned into a home. Inhabitants of the district speak of the pleasant impression it gave after the new tenants' advent, with its flowers and creepers, the three windows highly polished, and, hanging in one of them, a bird singing in a cage. On the flat roof of the house there was a railed-in gallery, with a magnificent prospect up and down the river. Here the male tenant was to be seen sitting for hours at a time, taking his frugal bread and cheese and porter, watching the fireworks in Vauxhall Gardens, or studying the dawn and sunset.

'The Admiral' kept a rowing-boat at the wharf, and whenever he came for it, Mrs. Booth (described by the boatmen as a big, hard, coarse, but not un-amiable Scotchwoman) was with him. It was these boatmen who declared that Turner was 'completely overshadowed' by the lady, and they tell how he would invariably consult them as to the weather before putting out on the water. If it was cloudy he would defer to Mrs. Booth with an apologetic "Never mind, Old 'un, we won't go far," and in the approving answer from her of "Very well, dear," they would be rowed over to Battersea Church or to the fields now forming Battersea Park. On other occasions he is spoken of as setting out with a sturdy stick for a day-long walk, and as speaking afterwards of his pleasant ramble "through the market-gardens and by footpaths to Brompton and Hyde Park"—where they were shortly afterwards to build the Crystal Palace, or Great Exhibition, as it was then known. The door

of Queen Anne Street remained at this period bolted
and barred, we are told, so we must assume that the
despairing Hannah Danby and her children had
been temporarily deposited elsewhere.

If by chance any former acquaintance did happen
across him in the Chelsea district, he got small change
out of the secretive painter. One such met him on
the early morning steamboat, *en route* for the City,
and asked him whether he resided locally. "Is that
your boy?" riposted Turner, pointing to the other's
son. Another, visiting The King's Arms at Cremorne,
and finding the artist cuddling a glass in the chimney-
corner, remarked: "I didn't know you used this house.
I shall drop in often now I've found out where you
quarter." Turner rose, frowning, put down his
tumbler, and hobbled to the door. "Will you?" he
mumbled, "I don't think you will," and disappeared
in high dudgeon.

Unless Mrs. Booth's putative husband was still alive,
it may seem strange that at this stage Turner did
not marry her, since they were so well suited. I think
the answer may be found in his Testamentary dis-
positions. He may have feared that as his wife she
would endeavour to nullify his intentions. There is
also, of course, an old proverb about shutting the
stable door. . . . He may even have considered it
would be rough on Hannah Danby. All we know for
certain is that he died a bachelor.

For two or three years at this stage he seems not
to have handled a brush at all. The pictures exhibited

—*Undine*, *Angel Standing in the Sun*, both vignetted, and *Hero of a Hundred Fights*—were assuredly painted earlier, and only now sent in to preserve the harmless fiction that he was still an active worker. As he still was, in respect of assiduity of observation, if not in output. He retained what Sir Walter Armstrong justly describes as 'the eye of a hawk and the patience of a German'. A passer-by along the Embankment by Westminster Palace noticed a small man sitting on his heels, gazing absorbedly into the river. Returning an hour later he saw the same squat figure in the same position, equally intent. It was Turner, studying the pattern of the ripples. His consuming passions were fame and money, but nature most of all.

During his silence and happily merely temporary passivity, the world was by no means standing still. One is stirred to excitement in more than one direction by merely summarising the events of those four or five short years—Röntgen was born, the planet Neptune discovered, telegraphic communication established with France, the Nelson column erected, and the British Museum opened. Louis Napoleon escaped from Ham, California had its gold-rush, and the thirty-seven-year-old Mendelssohn, short, dark, and strongly Jewish, conducted his setting to "A Midsummer Night's Dream" at the Philharmonic, London, before an audience which included Queen Victoria, the Prince Consort, and Jenny Lind. Within a year he was numbered in a death-roll of notabilities which included Captain Marryat, George Stephenson, D'Orsay's Countess of

Blessington, the Iron Duke, and Balzac. As for literature, not only was Robert Louis Stevenson born, but a whole library of masterpieces came into being: "Dombey and Son" and "David Copperfield", "Wuthering Heights" and "Jane Eyre", "Vanity Fair" and "Pendennis", "Uncle Tom's Cabin", "Lavengro" and Tennyson's "In Memoriam".

With Turner's unwonted idleness came back the itch to be busy. In fact, though he had decided to paint no more, force of habit was too strong and he could not stop himself. When the weather served he sat on the flat roof at work on what are called in France *pochades*, or rapid colour-sketches of transitory effects in nature. It is alleged that he would work on seven different studies simultaneously, transferring his attention from one to the other with the changes of the light and sky. Experts have discerned in these virtuoso-efforts the influence which originally inspired Pizzaro, Monet, and Renoir, just as Ruskin discerns in earlier works of his the seed-pod of the Pre-Raphaelite movement. On wintry days he worked in a tiny room with a window proportionately small, but out of which he could still study light and the effects of the sun upon the heavens. It was here that, as he felt his end approaching, he, in a St. Martin's Summer of inspired energy, produced his last four pictures: *Aeneas Relating his Story to Dido, Mercury Sent to Admonish Aeneas, Departure of the Trojan Fleet,* and *Visit to the Tomb.*

More perhaps than any others of his works, these

four pictures have excited precisely contrary judgments. The impartial student of the painter's life finds them dismissed as failures and acclaimed enthusiastically as his final and unsurpassed fruit of genius. Perhaps only Time can give the final verdict, but the account of how they came into being, from the lips of that unimpeachable authority, Mrs. Sophia Caroline Booth herself, cannot fail to be of interest in either critical camp. She was wont to perform the duties previously undertaken by his father, cleaning the Master's brushes, setting his palette, stretching canvases and varnishing the completed pictures. Towards the end the painter had not the strength to work continuously, but would rest on the bed in his work-room—with a bottle beside him—until his energy and inspiration were revived. The early morning was still a fruitful time with him; he would climb up to the railed platform on the roof, with a rug wrapped round him, paint for a while, and then go back to bed. Much of his last work was conceived in his dreams. Mrs. Booth speaks of his once being restless in the night and calling out excitedly for drawing materials, which she brought, and with which he made sketches for subsequent use.

Only very occasionally in the last few years did he venture outside Chelsea. In 1847 we find him suddenly appearing at the Academy Council, but avoiding his friends, and vanishing again. We hear of him dining with the Bicknells at Herne Hill, where D'Orsay made his portrait-sketch, and both Landseer and

Linnell, also present, made surreptitious studies of him. In the following year he visited his lawyer and added codicils to his will, in one of which provision was made for Mrs. Booth on a par with that already arranged for Mrs. Danby. On another occasion he bestirred himself to drive a keen bargain with the South Western Railway, to whom he sold the land adjoining his Twickenham villa. Incidentally, Sandycombe Lodge itself, the Queen Anne Street premises, and his two houses in Harley Street, still belonged to him when he died.

Hawkesworth Fawkes had continued sending the famous goose-pie from Farnley, for on Christmas Eve, 1849, Turner writes: 'Mother Goose came to a rehearsal before Christmas Day, having arrived on Saturday for the knife, and could not be resisted in my drinking your good health in a glass of wine to all friends at Farnley Hall, also wishing happiness and the compts. of the season to all.' He adds, continuing in the same unliterary style, more suited to a housemaid, 'Ruskin has been in Switzerland with his whife'(!), and concludes, 'I am sorry to say my health is much on the wain. I cannot bear the same fatigue, or have the same bearing against it, I formerly had—but Time and tide stop not—but I must stop writing for to-day, and so I again beg to thank you for the Christmas present.

> Believe me most truly
> > Your oblidged Servant.'

An equally characteristic missive is dated December 27, 1850, when the 'oblidged Servant' was 75:—'Many thanks for the Pie it is Excellent it only come in time to drink the health of all friends at Farnley and wishing the compliments of the season. . . .'

In that year he had for the last time both exhibited at the Academy, and attended Ruskin's birthday-party at Denmark Hill. He also arrived unexpectedly at a *soirée* given by the painter, David Roberts. In the Life of that artist we read that Turner was 'very agreeable, his quick bright eye sparkled, and his whole countenance showed a desire to please. He was constantly making or trying to make jokes; his dress, though rather old-fashioned, was far from being shabby'.

In the general camaraderie of the evening, Roberts vainly tried to elicit from Turner the secret of where he was so mysteriously living, since the Queen Anne Street house was shut up, and letters sent there went unacknowledged. Turner deftly evaded all queries, so Roberts, determined not to be outdone, saw him into his cab.

"Where shall I tell him to take you?" he slyly enquired.

Turner gave a knowing wink.

"Tell him to drive to Oxford Street, and I'll direct him further."

In the brief conclusion of our chronicle David Roberts again bears testimony. In 1851 Turner had not only ceased to exhibit at the R.A., but no longer attended its meetings. Knowing the advanced age and increasing feebleness of their comrade, the Academicians were gravely concerned as to his health and welfare, the more so as his whereabouts were unknown. It was considered that he might be offended by not having been elected P.R.A. upon the death of Sir Martin Shee, nor knighted like so many of his inferiors; so David Roberts, as a social intimate, was deputed to write to the Master at Queen Anne Street, and beg that they might meet. No answer was received for a fortnight, and his colleagues reminded themselves that Turner never even opened correspondence on the grounds that the writers 'only want my autograph'.

At last Turner unexpectedly appeared at Roberts' studio in Fitzroy Square. 'I tried to cheer him up,' says Roberts, 'but he laid his hand upon his heart and replied, "No, no; there is something here which is all wrong." As he stood by the table in my painting room, I could not help looking attentively at him, peering in his face, for the small eye was brilliant like that of a child, and unlike the glazed and "lacklustre" eye of old age. That was my last look.'

It was the last look of any of his compeers, for Jones had seen him earlier that day. At Chelsea, though it was evident his dissolution was at hand, he refused to credit it. It was as if he felt that not only his work, but he himself, was immortal. Against his wish and without his knowledge Sophia Booth summoned from Margate the Dr. Price who had known them both since the commencement of their association.

The medico arrived on December 18th, and thought it no kindness to conceal from Turner that his death could only be a matter of hours. Even then the dying man would not credit it.

"Go downstairs," he told the doctor. "Take a glass of sherry, and then look at me again."

Meantime Hannah Danby, who had heard nothing from her master for many weeks, was putting away an old coat of Turner's at Queen Anne Street, when she found a letter in the pocket which suggested that the missing man might be at Chelsea. I find it impossible to share with my brother-biographers the belief that her impulse to go and find him proceeded from any motive of sentiment. She was only human, and so was scared lest he might have willed his money elsewhere, probably to some calculating female-stranger. Whatever her motive, she trudged to Chelsea with another old woman as infirm as herself, and by describing the artist to the keeper of a shop where ginger-beer was sold, learned that a similarly odd old gentleman, known locally as Admiral Booth, was living with his wife in a cottage at Cremorne. Hastening there, she found the painter at his last, and sent immediately to Islington for Mr. Henry Harpur, a relative of Turner's on his mother's side, whom he had made an executor of his will. She doubtless considered she had thus put an effective spoke in Mrs. Booth's wheel.

That gentleman arrived the same evening, but the artist was too far gone to recognise him. In that appropriately squalid spot, all that was mortal of the man was passing. Delirious, he 'babbled of green fields', and friends long dead, of Margate and his fruitless early love. . . . Becoming unconscious, it was feared he would expire in the night, but on the morning of December 19, 1851, he woke at dawn, and in the presence of Mr. Harpur, Dr. Price, and Caroline Booth, tried to struggle from his bed to gaze once more upon the river which throughout his life he had so dearly loved, which he had depicted in his very first oil-painting to be hung in the Academy, and on the banks of which so much of his work was to find a home. When they tried to dissuade him he grew more insistent; they must wrap his rug about him and help him to his railed-in roof. The sunrise—he must see the sunrise! Fearful of the consequences of a refusal, they temporised by assisting him to the tiny window, and there, his dimming eyes lit by that dawn he worshipped, and which he alone among all painters could depict, he expired in their arms, with his sole creed upon his lips.

"The sun is God!"

CHAPTER XI

1851–6

THE first impulse of Turner's executor, Mr. Harpur, with the death of so great a man, was to conceal the scandal of his having died under an assumed name and in invidious circumstances. He accordingly arranged that the body should secretly be transferred to Queen Anne Street. The rumour that 'Admiral Booth' was not just what he seemed was already rife in Chelsea, for Mrs. Booth herself confessed that she had been unable to refrain from hinting here and there from time to time that her husband was really a great man in disguise.

The landlord of the King's Arms at Cremorne, who had known the dead man well as an almost-too-frequent customer, speaks of the removal of the body. He had observed a hearse outside the 'Admiral's' cottage, and had heard that he was dead. Soon afterwards the undertaker's men came into the bar for a drink, and while there, talked somewhat disparagingly of the place they had been sent to. The staircase, it appeared, was so narrow that they could not get the coffin up it, and had to carry down the corpse instead. They mentioned with surprise that the coffin was of lead and lined with satin, as if it were meant for a lord.

The death-mask, now in the National Portrait
Gallery, was taken; and one of the young Trimmers,
by this time grown up, writes with emotion of it:—

'Dear old Turner. There he lay with his eyes sunk
and his lips fallen in. He reminded me strangely of
his old father, whom, long years before, I had seen
trudging to Brentford market from Sandycombe
Lodge to lay in his week's supplies.

'On his calm face were written the marks of age
and wreck, of dissolution and reblending with the
dust. This was the man whose worse productions
contained more poetry and genius than the most
laboured efforts of his brother-artists; who was the
envy of his rivals, and the admiration of all whose
admiration was worth having. . . .'

By this test the admiration of The Times was not
worth having, for in a disparaging obituary, chiefly
dealing with the cash values of the artist's work, the
fatuous journalist contents himself with a brief comment
that 'although it would here be out of place to revive
the discussion occasioned by the peculiarities of Mr.
Turner's style in his later years, he has left behind him
sufficient proofs of the variety and fertility of his genius
to establish an undoubted claim to a prominent rank
among the painters of England'.

I delight in recording that the painters of England
themselves thought very differently, and were able
so to testify in a way that even The Times could not
afford to ignore. On December 30th Turner was
buried in the crypt of St. Paul's, next to Sir Joshua

Reynolds. The service was conducted by Dean Mil-
man, and the mourners included every artist of note
then in England, including the P.R.A., Sir Charles
Eastlake, Landseer, Mulready, Copley Fielding, Clarkson Stanfield, and Maclise. Among the throng of
private mourners was observed 'an elderly female,
heavily veiled', from which we can easily deduce
the highly natural presence of Hannah Danby, in
her customary big bonnet, the veil being doubtless
added on this public occasion to mitigate the dis-
figuration of her features.

The death, long expected, did not come as such a
shock to his friends, though at Farnley Hall the usual
goose-pie had just been packed up ready to send.
Ruskin was abroad, but his father lost no time in
repairing to Queen Anne Street to earmark works
for his collection in the event of a sale taking
place. Lord Lansdowne went with the same object,
and describes how, after ringing the bell, he was
standing in the fog on the doorstep when 'the old
woman in charge, looking up through the area railings,
took him for the cats'-meat man, and bawling up,
told him he needn't come again, "as the cats were
being got rid of".'

It was about the same time that young Trimmer
paid his last visit to the 'Turner Gallery', of the
desolation of which he speaks affectingly . . . the
dreary room of unfinished pictures, the damp, the dust,
the gloomy studio with its heaped canvases turned
face to the wall. Here were the idle colours, and

the almost hairless brushes, the silent flute, the cracked decanter with its single glass. In the dilapidated bedroom, with its leaking roof, he found the artist's travelling-library—Izaak Walton, Young's "Night Thoughts," and Horace in translation, beneath the dead man's gloves and neckkerchief.

Ruskin, on his return from abroad, received permission to reduce the chaos of drawings and sketches into some sort of order, and spent months of continuous labour in gratuitously sorting and systematising with two assistants 'upwards of 19,000 pieces of paper, drawn upon by Turner in one way or another. Many on both sides. Some with four, five, or six subjects on each side—the pencil point digging spiritedly through. . . . Some in chalk, which the touch of the finger would sweep away. . . . Others in ink, rotted into holes. Others (some splendid-coloured drawings among them) long eaten away by damp and mildew, and falling into dust at the edges, in various stages of fragile decay. Others worm-eaten; some mouse-eaten; many torn half-way through; numbers doubled (quadrupled, I should say) into four, being Turner's favourite mode of packing for travelling; nearly all rudely flattened out from the bundles in which Turner had finally rolled them up and squeezed them into the drawers in Queen Anne Street'.

The deceased's will came to probate, and revealed at last the true secret actuating the extraordinary double life of the great painter. The many years spent of his own choice in conditions of penury, his refusal of huge sums continually being offered for his work, even when such projected purchases were intended for National Collections, had been inspired by one sublime resolve—to make a free gift to the Nation, not only of all his paintings, drawings, sketches, and entire artistic output, but also the whole of his huge fortune so thriftily amassed.

The style of the Testament is as illiterate, diffuse, and marred by mis-spellings, as "The Fallacies of Hope" the diaries, letters, and all the other writings of the deceased, but his intentions are abundantly clear. After stipulating that his pictures *Dido Building Carthage* and *The Sun Rising through Vapour* should hang in the National Gallery between *The Seaport* and *The Mill* of Claude, the Testator directed that all his 'Leasehold and Personal Estates and property of every description whatsoever' (with the exception of certain minor bequests to two uncles and three nephews whom he hardly knew, and a small income for the support of Mrs. Danby and his children by her) should be devoted to a charitable institution, to be known as Turner's Gift, 'for the Maintenance and Support of Poor and Decayed Male Artists being born in England and of English parents only and lawful issue'.

That will was dated June 10, 1831, and two codicils in 1832, the first of which was signed but not witnessed, stipulated for the erection of a gallery 'to keep my Pictures together so that they may be . . . viewed gratuitously'; or, alternatively, if after five years no

such gallery is in being, then that his house at 45
Queen Anne Street should be utilised for the purpose,
and Hannah Danby be employed as Custodian at
£100 a year, with an additional £50 'for her assistance'.
Her 'nieces' are each left £50 p.a.; provision is made
for the annual R.A. dinner in celebration of the
Testator's birthday, and for the presentation of a
£20 medal for the best landscape every two or three
years.

A further codicil in 1848 revokes the bequests to his
relatives, and also to Hannah Danby, who, however,
is instead to be paid for the care of his pictures until
such time as the National Gallery shall have provided
special rooms for their reception, to be known as
'Turner's Gallery'.

The five years allowed to the National Trustees for
the fulfilment of his wishes is increased to ten in a
fourth codicil, dated 1849, in which Hannah Danby
and Mrs. Booth are equally bequeathed annuities of
£150; £1,000 goes to the Pension Fund and £500
apiece to two homes for Orphans. Turner also directed
that an additional £1,000 should be spent on the
erection of a memorial to himself in St. Paul's, and left
the whole of his property otherwise to 'Turner's Gift',
the institution for decayed artists mentioned in the
will proper. The latter codicils were properly attested
by 'Clerks to Mr. Harpur, Kennington Cross, Surrey'.

The will and codicils were proved on September 6,
1852, in the Prerogative Court of the Archbishop of
Canterbury, and the effects sworn under £140,000.

Unfortunately, the matter was not to end there. The vastness of the estate proved too much for the cupidity of that Exeter cousin who had only twice ever set eyes on Turner, the last time seventeen years before, and he contested the validity of the will on the grounds of the insanity of the Testator. Though this plea failed, the lawyers had by now got their grappling irons upon the money-bags, and were determined not to let go. The example of Jarndyce v. Jarndyce in "Bleak House", just then published, doubtless made them the more eager for another such opportunity, where, regardless of integrity or justice, litigation could continue year after year until all the money in the engineered dispute had been swallowed up in legal fees. Their contemporary, Disraeli, has pronounced that the barrister joys in 'illustrating the obvious, explaining the evident, and expatiating on the commonplace'. In the Turner Will Case, however, the gentry in wig and gown had the more difficult but none the less pleasurable task of obscuring, by every devious stratagem, the palpable wishes of the deceased. Faultily worded technically as the document may be (and let us not forget that one solicitor, if not two, had charged Turner professional fees for attesting it, and presumably checking it, before his death), the three simple facts in it that stick out a mile for any normally intelligent and reasonably honest man to read are that (1) the utmost which Turner ever meant to leave those strangers, his relatives, was £50 a year each, and even this bequest was revoked in a subsequent codicil;

(2) his mistresses and illegitimate children were to be properly provided for; and (3) that he intended the entire balance of the £140,000 he left to be devoted to the foundation and upkeep of a charitable asylum for indigent artists who were wholly English.

The legal leeches had their way. For more than four years the money that Turner had scraped together by laborious industry and grinding economies was recklessly squandered. Indeed, I suppose that Englishmen ought to consider themselves lucky that, thanks to the abysmal ignorance of lawyers on the subject of Art or anything that really matters, they did not appreciate the commercial value of the paintings in the will, else these also would surely have been sold to bring more fees. In March, 1856, the Vice-Chancellor at last gave judgment, and, needless to say, the man who made the money was permitted after death no voice in its disposal. The two main things he had planned and saved for were ruled completely out. His less-successful artist-brethren did not gain a penny-piece by his life-time of abnegation, for there was never any 'Turner's Gift', any more than there was provision made for his true dependants, whether children, Mrs. Booth, or Hannah Danby. Except for £20,000, free of legacy duty, pounced upon—wholly without justification, according to me —by the Royal Academy, the whole of the money left which had not adhered to the sticky fingers of the lawyers, together with his various houses, plates,

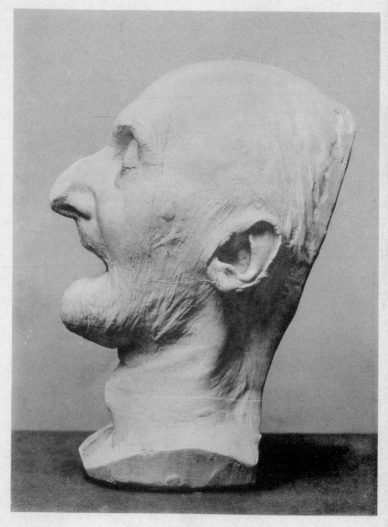

TURNER. DEATH MASK
(National Portrait Gallery)

engravings, and priceless copyrights, was handed, under the Statute of Mortmain, to an heir-at-law who was virtually a total stranger to the Testator, upon whose goodwill he had not the faintest claim.

The bequests as regards the artist's works were not, apparently, worth anybody's while to dispute, and the nation is the richer by more than three hundred paintings, to be seen in the National Collections, and countless superb drawings and sketches, sorted and arranged by the devoted Ruskin, now in the basement of the National Gallery.

The monument in St. Paul's, for which £1,000 had been allocated, eventually came into being in a statue by MacDowell, but, the man being dead, and his money dispersed, indifferent parties carved a wrong date on his tomb; just as, when some artists applied to put a memorial-tablet outside his birthplace in Maiden Lane, the Board of Works refused permission.

The fallacies of hope!—it is Turner's own phrase. But I cannot help remembering those other words of his, when he lamp-blacked *Cologne* out of kindness to Sir Thomas Lawrence. "It'll all wash off after the Exhibition," said he. Well, the wolves and vultures flocked round his corpse, and tore all the flesh from his bones. But they could only cheat him of his money and his life's ambition. After the Exhibition was over, Time washed away their dirt and his, leaving behind —his work, the essential Turner, bearing no more resemblance to 'the man in his habit, as he lived', than do those ashes in St. Paul's.

> 'Dust thou art, to dust returnest,
> Was not spoken of the soul.'

Those words of his contemporary, Longfellow, will never seem quite trite again.

THE END

BIBLIOGRAPHY

Adams, W. Davenport. *Dictionary of English Literature.* (Cassell.)

Anderson, John. *The Unknown Turner.* (1906.)

Armstrong, Sir Walter. *Turner.* (1901.)

Arnoult, L. *Turner, Wagner, Corot.* (1930.)

Bayes, Walter, A.R.W.S. *Turner, a Speculative Portrait.* (Bles, 1931.)

Bega. *The Turner Spell.*

Binyon, Laurence. *English Water Colours.* (A. & C. Black, 1933.)

Black, Ladbroke. *Some Queer People.* (Sampson Low.)

Boswell, James. *Life of Johnson.*

Burney, Fanny (Mme. D'Arblay). *Diary and Letters.*

Cooke, Sir Theodore Andrea. *The Water-Colour Drawings of J. M. W. Turner in the National Gallery.* (Cassell, 1904.)

Dictionary of National Biography. Many volumes.

Encyclopaedia Britannica. Many volumes.

Finberg, A. T. *The English Water Colour Painters.* (Duckworth.)

Gill, F. T. *Turner*, etc.

Girtin's (Thomas) *Water-Colours.* (The Studio, 1924.)

Green, John Richard. *A Short History of the English People.* (Macmillan, 1909.)

Hamerton, P. G. *The Life of J. M. W. Turner, R.A.* (Seeley, 1895.)

Hind, C. L. *Turner.*

Macfall, Haldane. *The Modern Genius.* (Jack, 1911.)

Monkhouse, W. Cosmo. *Turner.* (Gt. Artists Series, Sampson Low.)

Orpen, Sir Wm. *Outline of Art.*

Pendered, Mary L. *John Martin, Painter. His Life and Times.* (Hurst & Blackett, 1923.)

BIBLIOGRAPHY

Petrie, Charles. *The Four Georges. A Revaluation.* (Eyre & Spottiswoode.)

Piozzi. *Anecdotes.*

Rawlinson, W. G. *Turner's "Liber Studiorum".* (1906.)

Redding, Cyrus. *Past Celebrities.* 2 vols. (London, 1866.)

Ruskin, John. *Modern Painters.*

Swinburne, C. A. *Life and Work of J. M. W. Turner, R.A.* (Bickers, 1902.)

Tate Gallery Catalogue.

Thackeray, W. M. *The Four Georges.*

Thornbury, Walter. *Life and Correspondence of J. M. W. Turner.* (Chatto & Windus, 1877.)

Townend, Harry. *J. M. W. Turner,* etc. (1923.)

Watts, Alaric. *Liber Fluviorium.* (1853.)

Wedmore, Fredk. *Turner and Ruskin.* (Geo. Allen, 1900.)

Willenski, R. H. *English Painting.* (Faber & Faber.)

Wyllie, W. L., R.A. *J. M. W. Turner.* (Bell, 1905.)

INDEX OF PERSONAGES

229

INDEX

Brereton, Mrs., actress, 134
Brewster, Sir David, 146
Britton, J., publisher, 41
Brontë, Anne, 133
Brontë, Charlotte, 133, 210
Brontë, Emily, 133, 210
Brookfield, Charles, 176
Browning, Elizabeth Barrett, 103
Brummell, 'Beau': George Bryan, 134, 191
Burke, Edmund, 12
Burney, Fanny (Mme. D'Arblay), 17, 22, 191
Burns, Robert, 29, 64, 158
Byron, George Gordon, Lord, 64, 67, 89, 97, 133, 134, 148, 158,
    164

Cadell, Mr., bookseller, 70
Callcott, Sir Augustus Wall, R.A., 152, 201
Campbell, Thomas, 64, 158
Canaletto, Antonio, 46, 170
Canning, George, 154
Canterbury, Archbishop of, 222
Carlyle, Thomas, 172, 182
Caroline of Brunswick, 58, 141
Cervantes, Miguel de, 158
Chantrey, Sir Francis, 83, 101, 102, 110, 127, 132, 147, 155,
    174, 180, 193
'Charlie, Bonnie Prince', Charles Edward Stuart, The Young
    Pretender, 39
Charlotte, Princess, 58, 142
Chatham, Earl of. See Pitt, William the Elder,
Chesterfield, Lord, 20
Chopin, Frederic Francois, 148
Clarence, Duke of (afterwards William IV), q.v.
Claude of Lorraine, 39, 47, 87, 91, 92, 126, 140, 153, 199, 221
Clive of India, 20
Coleman, Mr., schoolmaster, 34
Coleridge, Samuel Taylor, 62, 172
Collins, Wilkie, 186
Colman, George: the Younger, 20, 60, 176

230

INDEX

Constable, John, 30, 179, 182
Cook, Capt., 11
Cooke, Mr., publisher, 108, 128–30
Cotman, Frederick George, 46
Coutts, Mr., Banker, 134
Cowper, William, 64, 158
Cozens, John Robert, 28, 46
Cromwell, Oliver, 104
'Crop-ear', pony, 99, 115, 121
Cuyp, Albert, 39

Danby, Hannah, 33, 81, 82, 84, 90, 94, 99, 104, 112–14, 117,
    118, 132, 133, 153–5, 162, 163, 168, 173, 180, 181, 208,
    212, 215, 219, 221, 222, 224
Danby, Sarah, 81
Dance, George (afterwards Sir Nathaniel Dance-Holland), 76, 192
Darwin, Charles, 103
Da Vinci, Leonardo, 164
Davis, Scarlett, 174
Dayes, Edward, 35, 36, 75
De Loutherbourg, Mrs., 98
De Loutherbourg, Philip, J., 46, 73, 88, 97, 101, 116
De Quincey, Thomas, 142
De Stael, Mme., 58
De Tabley, Lord (formerly Sir John Leicester), 61, 89, 99, 153
Devonshire, Duchess of, 15
Dickens, Charles, 24, 37, 108, 158, 165, 172, 176, 187, 193, 195,
    201, 210, 223
Disraeli, Benjamin, 176, 201, 223
D'Israeli, Isaac, 64
Dobson, Mr., architect, 41
D'Orsay, Count, 62, 192, 193, 209, 211
Du Fresnoy, writer on Chromatics, 146

Eastlake, Sir Charles, P.R.A., 219
Edward VII, 193
Egremont, George, Earl of, 99, 101, 102, 132, 179, 206
Elgin, Lord, 68
Eliot, George, 133

231

232

MADE & PRINTED IN GREAT BRITAIN
BY PURNELL & SONS, LTD., PAULTON (SOMERSET) & LONDON